No One Is Coming To Save You

NICKY MARSHALL

Published in 2024 by Discover Your Bounce Publishing

www.discoveryourbouncepublishing.com

Copyright © Discover Your Bounce Publishing
All rights reserved.

Printed in the United States of America & the UK.
No part of this book may be used, replicated or reproduced, stored in a retrieval system, or transmitted in any form or by any means, electronic, mechanical, photocopying, recording, or otherwise, without the written permission of the author(s).
Quotations of no more than 25 words are permitted, but only if used solely for the purposes of critical articles or reviews.

978-1-914428-27-2

Although the author and publisher have made every effort to ensure that the information in this book is correct at the time of going to print, the author and publisher do not assume and therefore disclaim liability to any party.
The author and the publisher will not be held responsible for any loss or damage save for that caused by their negligence.

Although the author and the publisher have made every reasonable attempt to achieve accuracy in the content of this book, they assume no responsibility for errors or omissions.

Page design and typesetting by Discover Your Bounce Publishing

CONTENTS

Foreword by Cally Stewart	1
Tip One	4
Introduction	5
Tip Two	12
Chapter One: The World Is Not A Safe Place	13
Tip Three	19
Chapter Two: Saving Myself	20
Tip Four	31
Chapter Three: Do You Need Saving?	32
Tip Five	40
Chapter Four: No One And No 'Thing' Can Save You – Here's Why	41
Tip Six	55
Chapter Five: The Vision, Part One	56

Tip Seven	70
Chapter Six: Your Wellbeing Toolkit	71
Tip Eight	92
Chapter Seven: Talking All Things Woo!	93
Tip Nine	113
Chapter Eight: What Is Resilience Anyway?	114
Tip Ten	120
Chapter Nine: More Work To Do!	121
Tip Eleven	143
Chapter Ten: The Big Vision	144
Tip Twelve	153
Conclusion: Our Journey Is At An End	154
Afterword by Sharon Critchlow	156
About The Author	158

About Discover Your Bounce 160

Other Personal Development Books 162

FOREWORD
BY CALLY STEWART

When I think of Nicky, the words that immediately come to mind are resilient, magickal and inspiring. Despite how cliché it might sound, I stand by my next sentence: Nicky is not just a survivor but a vibrant force of nature. This magickal woman has intentionally crafted her life to be the fullest, most authentic version of herself despite facing challenges that might have crushed others. Her journey is nothing short of inspiring.

This book is a testament to Nicky's unwavering belief in the power of transformation. It's more than a collection of experiences, it's a guide to finding strength, hope and magick in the most unexpected places. Nicky has poured her heart into these pages, offering not just her story but the powerful wisdom she has gained through years of navigating life's toughest moments. Whether you are at a crossroads, looking for inspiration or simply wanting to connect more deeply with yourself and the world around you, this book is everything you need.

What I admire most about Nicky is her ability to turn shit into manure, pain into power, struggle into purpose! She doesn't just survive, she thrives, and she does so with an infectious positivity that leaves everyone around her better for it. Nicky has faced trauma and adversity with a brightness of soul that refuses to be dimmed. She has an extraordinary gift for finding magick in the midst of chaos and she shares that gift generously in this book.

As you read through these chapters, you will find yourself on a journey - not just through Nicky's life, but through your own possibilities. She invites you to see the world differently, to embrace the unknown and to discover the unlimited potential within yourself. This book is not just meant to be read; it's meant to be lived.

Prepare to be challenged, uplifted and inspired. Nicky's words are not just a reflection of her own life, they are a call to action for anyone who has ever felt lost, broken or uncertain. In reading this book, you'll find a friend who understands, a mentor who guides and a beacon of hope that shines through even the darkest of times.

So, take a deep breath, open your heart and get ready to embark on a journey of self-discovery and transformation. Nicky's story is a powerful reminder that no matter where you've been or what you've faced, there is always a way forward - a way to bounce back, rise up and live your most authentic, magickal life.

Enjoy the journey.

NO ONE IS COMING TO SAVE YOU
NICKY'S TIPS TO SAVE YOURSELF
TIP ONE

Rocks, gravel and sand

When you are overwhelmed by everything you have to do, write down everything you can think of that is on your list. Next, take three highlighters (any excuse to get the stationery out, right?!)

Highlight your rocks: these are your most important tasks. You can only have three per day and one needs to be for your own wellbeing.

Highlight 'gravel' tasks – these are important, but not urgent. If they are still on your list after a few days they may upgrade to a rock.

Highlight sand: these are things you can delegate, perhaps you don't really need to do them…or they are the 'nice to have' tasks if you have headspace left over.

(Thanks to Liz Blackburn and Ruth Bruce for suggesting I share this tip)

INTRODUCTION

I have wanted to write this book for a while now. As a publisher, I love to help other people publish their books. Whether it's a business book full of thought leadership or a saucy fiction novel, I love to see people bringing their voice to the world. So often an author will say, "Why would people want to hear my story? I'm not special." My reply is always the same, "What you have to say is special and amazing. What you have to say is important."

When it came to writing my book, I was putting it off. I told myself I was so busy publishing other amazing books that I just didn't have time for mine.

At the end of 2023 I spent four weeks in South America with Mr M. We visited Brazil, Argentina, Bolivia and Peru and I can honestly say it was life changing. From spending time watching jaguars on the wetlands of the Pantanal, to sitting on a beach in Rio sipping from a fresh coconut. From creating crazy perspective pictures on the Salt Flats of Bolivia, to discovering Machu Picchu - every day was magical.

It was one early morning in the desert visiting the Stone Tree that it hit me.

I had been hiding from writing my book.

We were in a 4 x 4, being thrown about as the road system wasn't really a road, more like a dirt track with rocks on. We had hardly slept due to the altitude; we were at 4,500 metres, I had a massive headache; and it felt like my heart was skipping a beat out of every three or four. I couldn't sleep, so decided to meditate instead. I've been meditating for over 20 years and can pretty much meditate anywhere. I recently did a beautiful meditation to help me keep still in an MRI scanner, so a bumpy jeep was a doddle.

I decided to tune in to Pachamama, or Mother Earth, as we were in the middle of the desert, with the sun rising and nothing to see for miles but rocks and sand.

I first tuned into my breathing and asked Pachamama what I could do about my struggle with the altitude. She replied that, as Bolivians' lungs were twice the size of ours, all I needed to do was expand mine. 'Relax, expand and breathe' I heard.

So I did.

And my struggles eased. They didn't go completely, but I was much more comfortable.

The next part of the meditation was a bird's eye view of my whole life; my family, my friends, my marriage, my business. I am very good at practising gratitude, but perhaps at the micro level – the good things that have happened that day or that week. This was a helicopter view, of how wonderful and amazing it was to live my life at this time.

Over the years I have created many vision boards, and many of the things I wanted have happened… not overnight, but over a year or two. In this meditation I realised that every time I created a vision board, I had reaffirmed the wonderful life I already had. I have an amazing family, wonderful friends, a beautiful marriage and a business I am super proud of, but over the years I had made all of these my priority. They are so precious to me, but I had been the co-creator of this by giving them my time, energy and attention.

I have the energy of a small child and really good health. For sure I have the odd issue or a grumpy day (which I'm sure those around me find funny as they are so rare), but since a debilitating stroke 14 years ago I have really focused on my health, wellbeing and energy levels.

I was then shown my book.

Do you think, with the life I have created, that I have a message to share? Do you think that perhaps, someone in my past position or a similar place, might appreciate some helpful words? Do you think that perhaps it was time to listen to the advice I give everyone else?

When we arrived at the Stone Tree, I realised this was a magical place.

This place was in the middle of a desert surrounded by five volcanoes. The effects of various eruptions millions of years ago and the movement of tectonic plates had created a garden of rocks. The altitude of this place, combined with winds of up to one hundred miles per hour and temperatures of down to minus twenty had eroded away these rocks to create amazing shapes. You could just look around, take a few snaps and get back in the car, or you could look deeper and see the shapes of camels and faces of the ancients.

This place reminded me of Sedona, Arizona; somewhere very close to my heart and a big part of my spiritual awakening (more on that later). Within minutes

I had climbed one of the rocks, easily. It seemed my lung expanding meditation had worked! As I stood there looking around, I remembered how vast this planet really is, but also how small I had been playing. How time and nature never stand still, the land is always evolving and changing and whether we like it or not, so are we. We could be doing joyful activities, building relationships that nurture us and work that fulfils us. Or we could be head down in a world of busy, never questioning whether there is a better way.

It was on top of that rock, in that moment, that I decided to start my book.

Why you should read this book

In this book I will share some of my story; of how I discovered myself after life had lost me. This isn't an autobiography, but I feel this bit is important to set the scene.

Maybe you picked this book up out of curiosity, perhaps you are the type of person that loves to learn new things and hear new theories.

Perhaps you are at a turning point in your life, you have made some big changes and want to explore what is next for you.

Or perhaps everything 'seems' ok. You love your family, you're happy in your job and have everything you need… but it feels like there's something missing. You laugh, but not to your soul. You connect, but not deeply enough. You like yourself, but you can't look in the mirror and know that you fully love yourself.

Or maybe it's a bit of all three.

I'm a big believer in synchronicity, so for me if you are reading these words, there is a message for you and I would love to know what this book does for you.

You can start from the beginning and read through this book in linear fashion, or you can dip into a chapter that calls you. This is your time; this is your book. You do you. I hope as you go through, you experience an 'aha' moment, or write a few notes. Perhaps a few days after reading a passage, something happens and you react in a different way. I would love that.

This book is not written to look pretty on your shelf. This book is written to get coffee stained, to become dog eared, to start stories of your own adventures. Make it your own, I even give you permission to turn down the corners… not really! Okay, you can, but maybe try to look for a bookmark first.

NO ONE IS COMING TO SAVE YOU

Oh, and don't let the title put you off – I say no one can save you, but of course if you were dangling from a cliff, or in a burning building then of course someone can - in the moment. The kind of 'saving' I mean is in a sustaining, 'meaning of life' kind of way.

Nothing scary will happen by reading this book. However, if you absorb the messages woven through it, I will warn you, magic may happen.

NICKY'S TIPS TO SAVE YOURSELF
TIP TWO

Take back your power

Holding onto anger allows the person you're angry at to maintain their power over you. Getting rid of negative emotions sets *you* free from *them*.

(Thanks to Emma Rowles for remembering this one)

CHAPTER ONE
THE WORLD IS NOT A SAFE PLACE

My world appeared to be a very safe place.

I had a lovely childhood filled with love and laughter. My mum and dad clearly adored each other, and my brother and I were treasured. We didn't want for anything; any money worries as we were growing up were hidden and my parents worked hard to provide for us. Our house was always full of friends and laughter. From dancing around on a Sunday morning, to time spent with our grandparents and cousins. Our family was close knit and in particular I spent a lot of time with my maternal grandparents. Nan was so very wise, with a sense of mischief and I could do no wrong in her eyes.

As a stroppy teenager I would always find refuge at her house, armed with a rock cake and a cup of tea everything always seemed ok again. Gramp was a man of very few words, content to watch the world go by and smile at us all. If ever you needed anything mending, he would pop off to his shed for a bit of 'doings'. I have so much love for these amazing grandparents, who marvelled at everything I did. It's making my eyes teary just thinking about them and if I can be half the grandparent they were then I'm doing a great job.

We had family holidays and made so many memories we still tell the stories of today.

I was born in Bath and went to local schools. I made friends and I'm delighted to say I keep in touch with a few special friends from that time, today. I left school with O levels and got a job at Midland Bank. Again, I made friends and spent my time there progressing through the ranks.

When I was sixteen and still at school, I met my future husband. He was funny, handsome and appeared very confident. From our very first meeting he made me feel special. He was always calling me (on the landline, that had a cord so you had to sit in the hall to chat – in public). At the end of every date, he wanted to arrange the next and I thought I was the luckiest girl alive.

He wanted to get married and have children and so did I. We laughed a lot, spent every spare moment together and I didn't notice or think about the red flag moments for a second.

When he got protective or asked about my every movement, he told me that it wasn't me he didn't trust, it was everyone else. Soon I absorbed the subtle message that the world was not a safe place for me.

When we argued, it would often end in him hitting something or breaking something. Once he punched the fence next to my head. Nope, still no red flags, as I got an apology and he said he couldn't carry on living unless I stayed with him.

Of course, in 2024, knowing what I know now I would know that this is typical narcissistic and coercive control behaviour born out of his own trauma and upbringing. I would like to think that 2024 Nicky would have ended the relationship immediately.

But I come from a family of carers and problem solvers and I thought that, if I loved him enough he would grow out of it.

He didn't.

When we had our first daughter he danced in the street with delight, doted on her and was happy to do everything.

When interest rates rose and he was made redundant, we both worked hard to make ends meet. I took on extra shifts at the bank and he got night shifts at a garage. We were like ships passing in the night and we were both tired and snappy.

One early morning he came home and confessed to chatting to another woman. He said she had given him attention where I hadn't, and he had found her funny when I had been argumentative and grumpy. He said that he had come to his senses and realised it was a mistake. He wanted me, he wanted us to be a family and he wanted another baby.

I gave myself a hard time over being a crap wife, of taking him for granted and of course agreed to another baby, our plan was for two or three. Mortgage rates finally subsided, he got his old job back and I fell pregnant, so it seemed like we were on track once again.

How wrong I was.

When our second daughter was born, five weeks late but perfect and beautiful, I was over the moon. I couldn't wait to take her home and felt like the luckiest mum. It was only after the gas and air wore off that I realised my husband had left. It had been a long night, so I assumed he was heading home to catch up on sleep ready to look after our two-year-old.

The next day I couldn't wait for our daughters to

meet, so when Ami toddled in I helped her onto the bed so she could meet her sister. She was delighted and so attentive, that at first I didn't notice the absence of my husband. When I did look up, he was stood at the curtain with a face like thunder. When I asked what was wrong he said, "I'm not ok with it." When I asked what, he gestured at Kassi and just said, "It."

You see, he had wanted a boy. To be honest we both assumed I was carrying a boy as my pregnancy was so different. When a little girl arrived and I was delighted; he was sulky and disappointed.

And in that moment my marriage was over.

I didn't realise it at the time and it took a further eight years to leave, for a variety of reasons. I had years of undiagnosed period pain and heavy bleeding, brought on, I thought, by a long pregnancy and heavy baby. In fact, now I believe that as my life collapsed that day, so did my body.

I had a hysterectomy at twenty-nine, but still, I didn't leave.

You see, the world wasn't a safe place, it wasn't me but everyone else.

Whether it was guilt, or whether my husband knew I would leave who knows, but life after Kassi's birth became even more locked down. If I went out and said I wouldn't be late, by 9pm he was on the phone shouting, "Where the fuck are you, you said you wouldn't be late!"

He would calculate the time it would take me to buy groceries.

I tried very hard after my hysterectomy to fix my marriage. For two years I encouraged him to re-train in a new job in the hope that he would be happy. We decorated and improved our home, to the point that it was perfect. On the outside we had it all; the family, the house, the cars, the salaries but inside I was so shut down. When the girls were awake I was happy; when they slept I stared at a brick below the TV.

Christmas Eve 2001 was a turning point. We were all ready to go to a family party, with coats on heading out of the door. I don't even remember what was said, but my husband shouted at both girls, right into their faces, point blank range.

And something in me snapped.

Just six weeks later, I had a new home and my freedom, so you can breathe a sigh of relief, but I need to share a bit more of the story first.

NICKY'S TIPS TO SAVE YOURSELF
TIP THREE

Me or not me

Don't default to thinking you are the problem. It can be easy to take the blame for a situation when someone acts upset or negative. Our first reaction is usually to ask, "What did I do?" Remember there could be many reasons for that person's reaction, and the majority will not be of your making. So, ask yourself, "Me? Or not me?" The answer may surprise you!

(Thanks to Laura Barnett for remembering this one!)

CHAPTER TWO
SAVING MYSELF

No one was coming to save me. So I saved myself.

In truth, there were people who could have saved me. Who would have been horrified to know what my life was really like within the confines of my marriage.

The daily control, like working out how long it would take to get groceries and the "where the fuck are you?" call if I took longer.

The snide remarks and the complete ignorance of how hard I was working to study, be there for our beautiful girls and keep the house tidy (a little too tidy if you know the links between tidiness and my mental health).

The absolute mood swings, where in the blink of an eye and for reasons I could never fathom, his eyes would go from sparkly blue to cold, accusing grey and I knew there was shouting from him and appeasing from me on the horizon.

Did I tell anyone? No.

Of course, there was the girl talk, having a bit of a moan. And the occasional comment from my parents, which I brushed away with the stock phrase, "I'm fine." But how could I honestly, coming from parents who were and still are very clearly in love, admit that my marriage was worrying? And in truth, then, I didn't know quite how controlled I was. How far I'd spiraled into myself. How small I had become in order to fit in, and in becoming small, how little I really thought I deserved.

I had quietly worked away studying. Now here was something I could control and something I could get my teeth into. Something with a purpose; an end goal. I had always been crap (technical term) at maths and had to take a CSE and an O level at school to ensure I got a qualification. A wonderful teacher called Mrs Knight ensured I passed; she was funny, clearly loved maths and made everything sound easy. If you didn't understand one explanation, she would come up with another, and another, until one stuck.

With a one year old and a three year old I started college; just an hour a week doing RSA levels I and II in practical bookkeeping. I was over the moon to pass. I then went on to study evening courses in AAT

Accounting. On my return from college the girls were still up and the house was a shambles, but I kept going. I met Katharine then; we didn't know it of course, but we went on to be firm friends and thirty years later she is a massive part of my life. We could never fall out; she knows far too much!

Three years later I had AAT under my belt and embarked on my CIMA Management Accountant course. This was four years of home study, and as a person with undiagnosed ADHD I did struggle with the discipline of this. There were too many last-minute cramming sessions as I had failed to study properly and I had to work really hard at the maths parts of these exams.

At the same time as studying, when Kassi went to school, I registered with an agency for accounting jobs. My brief was specific: a maximum of twenty hours a week and no more than a twenty-minute commute. I was assured that they only ever got full time roles, but within two days the perfect job landed and I got it. I got two temporary and one permanent roles this way and in the end Daniel from the agency had to admit that there was something magical that happened when I was job hunting.

Of course, I knew nothing about the Law of Attraction then, but with my clear instructions and a belief that it would happen I always found a great job. From a rural map making company, to a young software company with the loveliest people, I gained not only work experience but a belief in my professional self. At work I was confident, funny, supportive… looking back, my natural self. At home I was quiet, submissive, subdued, small. When the girls were around I was attentive, loving and caring. When they went to bed I now needed to study – the perfect distraction and a 'safe' option as I stayed within the confines of our house.

When I rarely went out with friends this would create dissonance in my marriage. At first when I asked if I could go (even writing this makes a bit of sick rise in my mouth), it would be fine. A week before it would still be fine. The day of the event he would deny that I told him, sulk about me going and I would leave under a shadow. If I was home later than about half nine, I would get shouting phone calls – the friends I was with would give each other 'that look'; a mix of pity, anger and sympathy.

I didn't realise it at the time, but I was slowly saving

myself.

Four months before my final exams my company announced redundancies were being made and asked for volunteers. My manager assured me my job was safe, but I knew I had to apply. We had come back from our summer holiday (which was to be our last as a family) and I just knew and felt, with every fibre of my being, that I needed to leave. The reason I thought was obvious: four months' money, exams in three months, leaving a month to get a more senior job.

Straightforward.

The next morning on my first day of garden leave I took the girls to school, then switched on the TV to see one of the Twin Towers in New York had been hit. As I watched, the second tower came down.

That afternoon my beloved nan was diagnosed with terminal cancer and given three months to live.

I was numb.

I did the only thing I knew how to do and jumped into caring mode.

I would do the school run and go straight to the hospital to see my nan and get her ready for the day. When my mum arrived mid-morning, I would head home to study until the school run in the afternoon.

I had a lovely view from our lounge window, looking down a long garden with trees at the bottom. I set up a study (pasting) table in front of the window with room for all my books. Side note… anyone else need to do fifteen other things before they study? This did provide a great place to work, but also a great place to ponder. It was sitting at this table that I came to the realisation my thirteen-year marriage, and sixteen-year relationship, was over.

That reality scared me witless, but it wouldn't go away. I had tried so hard to make our marriage work, but some things just cannot be mended, including my heart. Rejecting our perfect daughter had broken mine that day and I had really tried to forget, move on, and ignore my feelings. Sitting at that window with some headspace allowed me to acknowledge what was really happening.

I had spent eight years studying and worked my way up professionally to assistant accountant from bookkeeper. I was confident at study and at work and here I was about to get my 'big job'. Company accountant with my own office and a big desk; I'd dreamed of this.

That scary space felt too big, too much. So I threw

myself into studying.

Then I threw myself into job hunting and got THE job: Company Accountant.

Then I threw myself into a massively challenging new role.

Then I threw myself into Christmas.

And then?

I refer you back to *that* moment. Christmas Eve. The look on my girls' faces as they were shouted at did something to me. It turned out that me being shouted at was ok, but not my babies.

That afternoon I casually looked at the property pages in the local paper and realised I could afford to rent my own house. Now I was qualified, with the revered job of company accountant, I had different choices. In that moment I felt free and then terrified. I put down the paper and tried to ignore that strong call for change.

We continued to nurse my nan as her health deteriorated and she quietly slipped away from us. Her cancer had spread to her brain and so most of the time she was somewhere else. One afternoon while in hospital, in her reality she was getting ready for a party and was frustrated and upset trying to make her dress.

So, she and I gathered the bed sheets until she was satisfied that she was ready and could nap. I then sat with the nurses and had a long cry; it was so unfair seeing the strong woman that had given me so much in this horrible state.

Eventually she was able to move back in with my mum and dad, who tirelessly looked after her, day and night with love and care. I helped as much as I could, and the girls and I visited often. We also had help from Macmillan nurses who were amazing and covered the nights, so my mum and dad could get a little rest.

I thought a lot about my nan's life in those final days. My nan and grandad had enjoyed a long and happy marriage and even though my grandad had died 8 years earlier, my nan missed him every single day. When I thought about my own marriage, I knew I would never have that. I felt driven in those final weeks, resolute that I needed to leave before she died; again, I knew it in my bones.

The night before I left, I visited my parents and nan, had a cup of tea and acted as if everything was normal. When mum popped out to the freezer to get something in for tea I followed.

"You might get a call tomorrow, Mum."

My mum looked puzzled.

"You see, I'm telling him our marriage is over and he will ring you to stop me."

My mum looked serious.

"Are you ok?"

"Yes," I replied.

"Do you need anything?"

"No, I'm fine," I said.

And that was it. We both went back into the house, we all chatted for a while and I left.

You see, I was ok and I didn't need anything. I hadn't realised it, but all the time I was studying, working my way up in my profession, mixing with people who saw the world differently, I had been saving myself.

I had grown in intelligence; I had become more confident. I had stopped believing that the world was not a safe place for me, in fact it was quite the opposite. I knew I was resourceful; you can't study, work and bring up two energetic humans without learning a trick or two! I had been through surgery to heal my ailing body and now felt physically strong. I had connected with my spiritual self along the way (more of that in chapter seven) and felt in tune with myself and the world around me.

I had woven into being a new version of me, who deserved a new reality and was now going to get it.

And so, just six weeks after the Christmas shouting incident, I had a new home and a new life.

It wasn't easy.

At my nan's funeral my now ex-husband paraded around as the injured party telling everyone he didn't understand why I had left.

When we told the girls we were splitting up, he sat them down and told them that, "Mummy doesn't love us anymore," rather than the gentler way we had rehearsed. It took them a while to see what was actually happening and of course I took them with me to our new home, but I had to hold strong while lies were being created about me.

Even though we had a new home, it didn't feel like my own space as he would knock the door at 6am knowing the girls would let him in. I would jolt awake being threatened and menaced – in a quiet voice so no one else in the house could hear.

And then there were the death threats.

Of course, none of his family believed me at first, but he would ring and tell me exactly what would happen if I tried to take the girls away from him.

Sidenote: this wasn't ever my intention.

It was only when I texted his brother during one particularly threatening phone call to come down and hear for himself did I finally get believed. As I turned the phone onto loudspeaker I watched the colour drain from his brother's face. I still didn't get any support, but at least someone had heard, and I didn't feel like I was going mad.

Nothing was going to stop me; I had a purpose and I loved the new space I was creating. I didn't quite know what I wanted yet, but I sure as hell knew what was no longer for me.

My family and friends were wonderful during this time. I sofa surfed a bit, cried a lot and partied a bit – even though everything felt weird. I was grieving for my nan, grieving for the life I thought I had planned, and grieving for the version of me that had been through so much. At the same time I was discovering this new version of me, who had multi-coloured hair and a thirst for adventure. Who could do scary things and venture to new places. Who was creating a new life for herself and her girls that was safe, and fun and drama free. A place where no one needed saving.

NICKY'S TIPS TO SAVE YOURSELF
TIP FOUR

The polite rebuke

Sometimes people say mean things, or slip in a passive aggressive comment. Look said person in the eye with a smile and say, "I'm sorry I didn't quite catch that, what did you say exactly?" The first comment may have been an unconscious reaction, but if someone repeats their comment it's time for action. Usually though, the response is, "What I meant to say was…"

CHAPTER THREE
DO YOU NEED SAVING?

The world is a bit broken and a lot of us are a bit broken too.

We live in a time where there are more people than ever, with more gadgets and tech than we could have before dreamed of. If you landed here in a time machine from 1970, can you even imagine how that would feel?

Three TV channels have turned into three thousand. We now turn to a screen rather than a book to get our knowledge. Our news usually breaks on social media first.

We can travel anywhere in the world virtually before we ever get on a plane. We can learn hundreds of languages from our phones and they now live in your pocket not on a table in the hallway. Hardly anyone uses their phone to make an actual call, but most people have them glued to their hand or sticking out sideways from their ear!

If you want to decorate a room, you can create a model of that on your phone or see yourself with a new hair colour or outfit. Looking a bit tired and want to snap a picture? Throw on a filter and no one will know. Too ill to go into the office? No worries, you can dial in!

In creating a better world, we have created overwhelm.

Our young people drink less, hardly smoke, meditate and know all the facts about mental health – and yet a large proportion of them are struggling. In creating this 'better' world of safety and opportunity have we taken away the resilience brought about by hardship? In a recent workshop on happiness, one young attendee didn't know where to start, for fear of getting it wrong.

Our under-50s men have suicide as the biggest killer despite all the publicity and mental health knowledge available. It seems that having a profession, a family and a relationship is no longer enough to bring us feelings of happiness and fulfilment. It hurts my heart that in times of deep crisis human beings are still unable to reach out and say, "I'm not ok."

Our older people are being side-lined in the race for

more technology. On a recent call to our local council when my dad said he was unable to use a computer the reply (which was of course denied when I complained) was, "tough!" My parents now don't drive into the town they have lived in all of their lives, as they can't pay by cash to park and can't yet get to grips with the app.

Loneliness is not only affecting older people, but young people too. In an age where you can shop online for absolutely everything, from your clothes to your food, we no longer spend time in our towns. When I lived in Weston on the outskirts of Bath, I would often see the women in my street popping to the village every day for a few 'bits'. What they were really going for was conversation and connection.

And then there's menopause. In times gone by women went through 'the change' and my impression was they had a few hot flushes and then their periods stopped. What I failed to understand - and still don't fully - was the intricate hormonal dance that was occurring. In 2024 this is a bit unreal as you would assume (wrongly) that everyone would be aware of what would happen during menopause, whether going through it or supporting someone else, in order to be fully prepared.

This isn't a book on menopause, and I stress that am no expert, but in brief for anyone who may go through it or support someone in this stage of life:

Your oestrogen and progesterone levels drop, in chaotic fashion, leaving you suddenly with elevated cortisol levels,

Oestrogen is in every single cell in your body, until it's not and then everything changes. From bad breath, changed body odour, vaginal dryness, failing eyesight. There are over forty-two symptoms of menopause, and counting – and every woman's experience is different.

Your body turns to your testosterone to mix with a protein to make a version of oestrogen – leaving you with reduced testosterone, which can cause reduced confidence and no belief in yourself.

Your melatonin levels drop, so sleep becomes harder or impossible, for about two years if the average of my peers is anything to go by. I had a two-year stint of 'wandering the halls' between the hours of 2am and 4am, despite being a sleep expert.

You present to a GP as depressed, so unless they have up to date knowledge, which sadly a lot do not, they will treat you as such.

Whether to take HRT or not and what supplements

can help is still a lottery and you may disappear down a never-ending Google rabbit hole trying to work it out. I decided not to take HRT, but in hindsight and with several probable menopause related health challenges under my belt I probably should have.

My advice? Find yourself a well-trained menopause clinician and get educated on what is going on for you.

Back to our broken world.

Our schools are broken.

They often cannot offer safety and support to our neurotypical children, so is it any wonder our neurodivergent children are struggling? I am seeing too many wonderful parents going through hell to get the right support for their neurodivergent children.

They don't offer a supported place for our teachers to educate our children.

Home schooling, world schooling or unschooling can be wonderful alternatives for our brilliant little ones, but it can still be frowned upon. Or if you home school you can still, in 2024, be labelled a 'housewife'.

Our National Health Service is broken.

I have had first-hand knowledge of how amazing and brilliant our NHS is. I have also seen too many exhausted doctors, too many nurses scrambling around for the right equipment and too many people in pain waiting until the early hours for help.

Our political system is broken.

This is one I am really not going to go into, but as I type we have an election looming, and all I see is people trying to discredit and ridicule the other parties. The media is fuelling and adding to the fire and it feels like a circus. In my fifty-four years on this planet, I have seen governments come and go and every time there are unfulfilled promises.

Our society is broken.

To be able to live somewhere safe and feed your family is no longer a given. Some two parent families are unable to afford a house to live in, or food to eat. Homeless numbers are rising. Hate crimes are rising; despite there being more open discussion around gender, sexuality and race there are still people being bullied and hurt by others who fail to celebrate or even accept difference. Knife crime is on the rise and the heart-wrenching headlines send chills as we hug our children ever closer.

I could go on…

Let's get back to social media. Everyone is having the best time ever and you are missing out, right? On your best day ever you can be genuinely pleased for everyone, but on your worst day? It feels like everyone else knows what to do and you don't. It feels like you are missing out. It feels as if life is passing you by and there is nothing you can do to stop it.

Let me give you a hug. My hugs are famous!

Social media and money are similar, in that they are an energy that adapts to the beholder. Both can be a powerful tool; they can educate, inspire, realise and bring gratitude. They can also poison, depress, mask, fake and mislead.

That's the thing about energy, it's behind everything we do and everything we see. And in today's fast-paced, ever-changing and demanding race to life we can lose our energy to a world of overwhelm. We can feel like an imposter, we can feel beaten, and it can be a hard place to lift ourselves out of.

So as I write, yes, you may need saving.

But I'll let you in to a secret; we all need saving at one time or another. The saviour may not arrive on a shining steed and save the day. They may not arrive at the exact time you need them like in the movies. And they certainly won't bring a guaranteed happily ever after.

Read on through chapter four to read all about who or what won't save you - and then we get to the fun stuff I promise!

NICKY'S TIPS TO SAVE YOURSELF
TIP FIVE

"I'm calling in the next version of myself"

It can be easy to wait for the 'right' time, or to assume there will be a cloud clearing moment where the angels will herald in a new version of you. Perhaps you just need to own it, and call in your upgraded self when *you* feel the time is right.

(Credit to Rosie Millward for the reminder)

CHAPTER FOUR
NO ONE AND NO 'THING' CAN SAVE YOU – HERE'S WHY

As you read through this book you will learn about the times when I thought I needed saving and when ultimately, I saved myself.

There are times, moments, when we look to someone or something to save us. When we lack our own energy, have lost our way, or reached some kind of crisis point in our life. These are the times when we usually look for some magic wand or quick fix. This may provide some relief or distraction in that moment, but it's usually not the thing we were looking for.

So here is what won't save you…

A guru

Gurus can spin a good yarn and give you the impression that their way is the quick fix or magic pill you are looking for.

They may look like they are living that charmed life and have everything.

I have been shatteringly disappointed by so many gurus in my quest for the meaning of life! I have usually succumbed to their charms when I have lacked my own energy or confidence – or both! I have spent the money, gone to the workshop, bought the book. I've even hired them to speak at my own events, only to find that they didn't deliver one jot and in fact just made me cross with myself for falling for the shiny smoke and mirrors routine!

Let me distinguish gurus from amazing, genuine and humble people that have done the work, studied their craft and have a real passion for helping you. They won't give you false claims. They *will* have credentials that speak for themselves, they will be clear about the work it will take if you work with them and how long it took them to craft their own skills.

A relationship

Oh boy did I get the t-shirt trying this!

After leaving my first husband I embarked on the dating game. At thirty-two years old, I had been in a relationship as long as I'd been out of one. I was excited to find someone also on a spiritual path… and a little terrified!

I will use the nicknames given by my then work colleague Andy:

Gandalf

He was a spiritual healer and medium, with a string of prestigious qualifications. He opened doors and was witty and charming, but controlling and narcissistic in an intellectual and subtle way that took me a while to identify.

Migraine Boy

Quite fun, mostly normal, but would always cry off with a migraine just before a date, which I think was code for, 'I've got a better invitation from my rugby mates!'

Yorkie Man

Now I still have a soft spot for him. He was funny, genuine and made my girls giggle. He had big dreams and I really hope he achieved them. When we met, he was a long distance lorry driver and we had hours of nice chats. Our dates though? He would forget and do something else instead like take his mum shopping –

true story! Looking back, the reality was he was bruised and hurting from a previous relationship and not able to give me what he couldn't give himself.

After one last 'no show' moment I decided that unless I could find a 'normal' human being, I would become a nun.

What was really going on?

In all of these encounters and the times in between I was learning about myself and the world. I was learning what I wanted – and what I didn't! I was learning who I was and what I liked about myself. It took a while. In the longer term I learnt to love myself, as a wonderfully imperfect woman and a perfect work in progress.

The day after my thirty-fourth birthday I met Phil (or 'Sebastian' if you have read my earlier book *Tabby Turns the Tables*). He didn't need saving and he wasn't trying to save me. We had both done the inner work, in different ways, and twenty years later he still keeps me guessing, makes me laugh and we share in many adventures.

Do I ask for his help or opinion? Of course! Do I rely on him for stuff? Sure! If he wasn't around could I save myself? Absolutely!

An addiction

Whether it's smoking, drinking, gambling, over-working, sex, shopping, or anything else that is a compulsion, vices are initially a distraction and eventually a crutch. We tell ourselves we can stop any time, but in reality we need that buzz to fill a void. If we stop – what do we put in its place? I'll get to that.

A shiny object

Oh boy, these are fun! When life doesn't work, or we know we are unhappy, or we realise that a change is on the horizon, shiny objects can provide a wonderful distraction. For example:

A holiday

A house move

A tattoo (or two!)

A new business venture

A new car

A new relationship (see above)

A health kick

I could go on. It's like having a wound and adding a plaster, but then when the healing needs to happen, you add another… and another… and another…

When really you should rip them all off and let it breathe to let the healing begin.

It may sting.

It may be a shock.

It takes bravery.

But in the long run, it's the enduring, solid solution that brings with it proper, enduring healing, understanding and a better relationship with yourself.

In the following chapters I have some things to try that may indeed help you save yourself. I have been on a self-development journey for over three decades now and I like to think I have learnt some stuff. Tips, techniques, philosophies and life hacks. Some discovered by accident and some by reading, sitting with and following some amazing people. Some through my own experience and some through times when life really didn't work for me.

We all need to find our own version of how to save ourselves. What works for one person may not work for another and what works in one instance may not work in the next. In my business I have taught wellness workshops and conducted mentoring for many thousands of people - all beautiful, amazing and unique.

In times of stress, some people sleep less and some

sleep more.

Some people eat less and some more.

Some people talk nineteen to the dozen and others go silent.

We all 'life' differently and will come to our own conclusions on what works in different ways. Our company is called Discover Your Bounce because we all need to find a way of bouncing, or getting back on track, that works for us. Then we can get out and try, be adventurous and do things that scare us, safe in the knowledge that if it all goes wrong, we can recover.

It may take time, we may sulk, pout and lick our wounds, but find a way back to balance when the time is right.

At this point I need to add a caveat.

I am possibly the most annoyingly positive person you will meet. I'm a 'find another glass' rather than half full or half empty girl. I will always cheerlead, cajole and encourage you to be the very best version of you that you can be.

I do have a magic wand, but there are times when there is no magic fix.

In 2010 I suffered a life and body altering stroke after a scuba dive. I lost the use of the left side of my body, had no strength or feeling in my arm or hand, no strength in my leg, reduced speech and memory - I was totally knocked for six. I couldn't drive my car or run my business – one that was only twelve weeks old.

That was a very dark and painful time in my life that I never want to repeat.

I have two beautiful children that live with chronic illness and try as I might I have yet to 'solve' that. I have friends with disabilities and mental health challenges, and I have not been able to 'fix' that either.

I know wonderful people that go through the most horrendous, gut wrenching life challenges and as much as I can sit with them, send them memes and give them hugs I can't take their pain away.

These amazing people are the most ingenious, inventive and inspiring humans that I know. They have a grit and determination, a way of digging deep, and they are also there to lend a hand and offer support whenever others are in need.

After the initial shock of the stroke, the pity party and the tears, the stark realisation that this wasn't an easy fix, and the scary realisation that I may lose my dream, there was a moment when I decided to get my life back. Not the old one; that particular version had caused enough stress for a stroke!

A new version.

One that was sustaining, health giving, life-affirming, with purpose and flow and fun. I called it Operation Goddess.

Why saving yourself is a good thing

To show you what magic can happen when you save yourself (or just for your amusement), here are some circumstances when I have looked to be saved and in fact learnt to save myself.

When I had just got used to being a single parent, I grew tired of the close proximity of my ex-husband. I moved with my children to a cute house in the country. Corsham is a lovely village with some shops, a few pubs and not much else, but I loved it. Initially my mum had forbidden me to move – she said, her exact words, that she wouldn't be able to save me if anything went wrong.

I said I was thirty-four and so could no longer be forbidden.

One sunny afternoon I was taking laundry in a big basket out to the washing machine in the garage. I had been busy doing my usual flitting about and was no doubt distracted. As I pulled up the garage door, which was on a spring, I failed to move my head and the door whipped up and smacked me hard under the jaw.

In that moment of disorientation, pain and panic, I realised that my parents would normally have been a twenty minute drive away but they were away for the weekend. I didn't know anyone in the village yet and so had no one to call.

Instead, I wobbled my way indoors, calmly asked the girls to get some paracetamol and told them to ring 999 if I fainted or went weird (they were teenagers and so capable of this).

***

When Phil and I first got together he couldn't wait to take me skiing, his favourite holiday ever. I was so excited!

In fact, it was the most terrifying, soul-destroying experience of my life!

I had this image of being a ski bunny carving my way down the mountain by day and living the high life of Après Ski by night.

The reality was my fear of heights raged as there were so many edges (on a mountain, who knew?). Snow is really slippery (again, shocking) and so stopping is REALLY HARD. And even though Phil tried to look after me, there were times when I was standing at the top of a precipice (literally) and had to find my own way down. I adopted my now famous mantra of, 'I am safe, I am well, I trust myself', learnt to breathe and sang to distract myself. It's fair to say that I had more lessons than the average person to finally get it, but get it I did.

Am I now a ski bunny? Nope! I do love skiing though.

***

In my early days as company accountant, I had the job of my dreams. My own office, responsibility and a nice salary. It was also terrifying! The person before me had left under a cloud and there had been no one doing the job for eight months. The external accountants had sent someone for a day, once a month, but the accounts were a real mess.

Every night I would scoop the contents of my desk into my bag, collect the kids, feed them and spend some time together. Around 9pm I would then pour a glass of wine, empty my bag and plaster post-it notes over everything so that I had some kind of order and a plan for the next day. This went on for months.

***

The first Father's Day after I had left my first marriage, I tried to make time for the kids to see their father and he had been vague and dismissive. At lunchtime I had a call from him asking, "Where the fuck are you? I want to see my children!" When he found out I was at lunch with my own lovely dad, family and partner he was incensed. We drove home and I knew he would be waiting. I felt sick and scared, but tried to keep calm and made light of it for the kids.

When we got there, he shouted, gesticulated and threatened and every plea to keep calm for the children's sake just made him worse. My then partner hid behind his car during the whole thing.

I stood helplessly as their father grabbed both of their hands and put them in his car. I went over to talk to them and he yelled, "You touch that door and you are dead!" I did it anyway.

I opened the door and he came flying towards me. I kept my hands behind my back so he could see I wasn't trying to get them out, so thankfully he stayed away. I calmly asked two very white-faced children if they were ok to spend a bit of time with their dad, as he was upset that he hadn't seen them yet; they nodded.

I then stood back, frozen, as he swore in my face before speeding away.

My partner said it would be fine, that he would calm down once he got the them home and promptly left too. I was now alone.

I had a cry and a shake, before ringing the police and asking their advice. He did return the kids by bedtime so I didn't have to call them again, but I did call on my solicitor and put plans in place so he couldn't come within 100 metres of me again.

***

Take a moment here and remember the times when you have saved yourself. The times when you have faced something scary. Perhaps you looked for external help and there was none. You are here reading this book, so you must have found a way through.

Sometimes the way to save yourself is hard. Messy. Scary. Soul-destroying. But it's worth it. In trying to find your own way you will find out so much about yourself. You will make mistakes, of course. You will hopefully laugh at a few of them, or at least learn to come to terms with them. Some things you won't be able to fix and that's okay. Sometimes you will hurt someone else, perhaps that's unavoidable. The point is if we are trying, we are learning.

Here's how I would like to help.

In the following pages I hope you find a nugget or two, perhaps a blueprint or a plan; a spark or an idea that will help you create the most toe-curlingly happy, sublimely delicious and sparklingly wonderful version of you, whatever you decide that looks like.

NICKY'S TIPS TO SAVE YOURSELF
TIP SIX

Lost items

It can range from really annoying to upsetting when things, or pets, go missing. Using the golden thread method has been a great resource over the years. Imagine a golden thread running from your heart to the thing or spirit you have lost. Tie a bow around them/it and gently tug them back to you. Repeat as often as you like.

(Thanks Michelle Armitage for the nudge.)

CHAPTER FIVE
THE VISION, PART ONE

I'm writing about your vision in two stages; a place to start and then a second round after I've shared a few skills and techniques. Creating a vision, for me, has been instrumental in creating the life I now enjoy and so I want to give it my proper attention.

'If you don't build your dream, someone will hire you to build theirs.' Dhirubai Ambani

Isn't that the truth? I have been swept along by other people with a strong vision in the past and in that moment been totally excited by what they were trying to achieve. After a while, I became exhausted and uninspired, realising that I had spent a lot of energy on something that I didn't totally believe in.

Of course, we can work on shared visions and projects but there must be an alignment, a win/win if you like, so that we can keep up our momentum.

I have read *The Secret*, *The Celestine Prophecy* series and also *The Law of Attraction* by Esther and Jerry Hicks. I have sat in the same room as Mike Dooley, Gregg Braden, Iyanla Vanzant, Bruce Lipton, Sonia Choquette, David Hamilton and Wayne Dyer (if you don't recognise these names, look them up – every single one has made a big impact on my life). I have read so many books and been to so many workshops and seminars. For around twenty years I was a sponge, soaking up spiritual knowledge.

Knowledge will only get you so far, you need to implement too.

For a while I was the student, learning theories and experiencing snippets of enlightenment in the classroom. I was so inspired, so excited, so refreshed. All of this was so new to me and I was meeting people who thought in the most amazing ways.

I recently came to the realisation that I had never had role models growing up who could show me the life I am now living. My dad had his own business from when I was ten and he is still my hero. He showed a bravery and belief in his business that allowed him to create an amazing lifestyle for us, his family. He has now retired at eighty-five, having started work at fifteen

- for seventy years he has worked so very hard. I love and admire him for that.

But I never saw a woman building her own business. I never had experience of entrepreneurs who had multiple businesses. I spent my time around people with quite a narrow, fixed view of the world and thought I needed to choose a 'job for life'.

After all those teachings, I knew I needed to strike out in my own way, to create a business that I was passionate about. Again, I had such a strong calling, I had received such powerful healing and transformation that I knew I wanted to pay that forward and help others.

In 2008 when I left my company accountant role to re-train in reflexology and Reiki and started to read Tarot professionally, can you imagine what my family thought!

Roll forward to 2010 and I combined my love of therapies with my other dream – to run my own coffee shop. The idea was to create a place where people could find sanctuary, whether that was just grabbing a quiet cuppa, receiving a holistic therapy or learning something new. But in 2012 I closed The Witches Brew; the business that had been my vision, but also the one that could have killed me. The coffee shop element is still trading today, and the holistic element I incorporated into the mentoring programme that we deliver through Discover Your Bounce. Last year I resurrected The Witches Brew brand as an online membership for women who are developing their spiritual self.

I knew when we closed that I no longer wanted a 'bricks and mortar' business, that I didn't want to work from the same place and I wanted more flexibility in my hours. I would not have arrived at that conclusion without starting that business.

What is your vision?

Do you have a clear plan? Can you explain, in detail what it looks like? Can you feel it? Does it give you butterflies and goosebumps?

If not, you are not alone. For some people their vision is to get to 5pm, for others the weekend. Some people are unaware that they need a vision and perhaps they don't.

But if you do want more, if you have a feeling that there is more to life, then you are right. If you feel you are being called to do more, have more, experience more, then the ideas I'm about to share are for you.

A caveat

If you work through these ideas and create your own strong vision, read the next few chapters too. I have seen so many excited puppies burn out by taking a massive idea and jumping straight in without preparation; I have done this a few times myself. In fact, in my first business my nickname was The Puppy!

A second caveat

If you want to share your vision, do so wisely. Choose people that will cheerlead, get excited with you and encourage you. Avoid:

Buzz Killers

Fun Sponges

Neg Ferrets

Negative Nellies

Energy Vampires

Indeed, avoid anyone who sucks through their teeth, frowns or tries to point out what could possibly go wrong.

Visions are like new neural pathways, or a weak muscle you work on in the gym. In the beginning they are fragile, wispy and delicate. As you use them, repeatedly work on them and gain experience they will get stronger. In the early days they can get absorbed into something else, but keep going and they will become strong, like oak tree roots.

Modelling

If you have an idea, but no thought of where to start, look for someone who is already doing it. You will, of course, find your own unique way but it's good to get ideas of what works – and what doesn't.

With the advent of the internet and Google we can get amazing ideas for our business, our life, our living space, our bodies, our health… if you want to create anything you can drop a few search terms in and get started.

Create your vision – option one

The Law of Attraction is a belief system or philosophy that believes there is The Universe. I put this in capitals as it's a living energy. In simple terms the law states that energy flows where attention goes, that The Universe and energy follows your foremost thought. That what we think about, we bring to life.

So if you are worrying about bills and not having any money, you will be given experiences that deplete your finances.

If you think and dream of a particular car, then you will attract it to you.

There are many laws in Esther and Jerry's book and if you want to look at this in detail their books are worth a read.

I love a good analogy, so think of The Universe as an algorithm. On Facebook and other social platforms, companies invest millions into working out what we want. They analyse our behaviours, monitoring what we click on. Marketing companies do A/B testing to see what excites us.

I like to think that The Universe works like this. What we pay attention to and spend our time doing, we get more of. It's not discerning – it doesn't choose between good or bad. Wherever we 'click', we see more.

Take a few minutes to assess your 'life algorithm', where have you been spending your time of late? Have you been doing things you love and talking positively? Or doing stressful things and using negative language? If it's not been a fun ride, no judgement is needed here, I believe what we notice we can change, if we choose to.

Create your vision – option two

The reticular activating system in your brain looks for what you talk about and think about. If you love a particular pair of red shoes, or wear red shoes a lot like my business partner Sharon Critchlow, then you will be attracted to more red shoes like a moth to a flame. In fact, you may become known as the speaker that wears red shoes - right, Sharon?!

So, by being clear on your vision and spending time thinking about all the intimate details of what you will do and how it will feel, you can fire up your own neurology to spot any opportunities to bring your vision to life.

Which theory do I adopt?

Both.

I love mixing the scientific and the spiritual. I love experimenting to see what works for me and I encourage you to do the same.

By getting clear on what I want I have manifested a wonderful trip to Sedona in Arizona, a writing and speaking career, the exact holiday home of my dreams - even my husband! How did it work? Who cares?! Am I living the version of life that I dreamed about in 2012? Yes, I bloody well am!

I have been encouraged to learn what works for me and I encourage you to do the same. If something doesn't feel right, drop it – there will be another way.

Fixed versus growth mindset

Once you start playing with this it may really open your eyes. I find that with anything new – once I see it I can't un-see it. You may start to observe those around you and those you meet and quickly see which mindset they have adopted.

Fixed: you must work hard for everything you get. You can't change your experience. You work hard for 45 years and if you're lucky retire, get a watch, do the garden for a few years and then die. If you fail at something then give up; it wasn't meant to be.

Growth: I can change my reality. If I fail, I learn and try again. I can always adopt new ways and new ideas; I can learn from others. I can ask questions and gain a new perspective.

I have learnt a lot by reading Dr David Hamilton's books. In *How Your Mind Can Heal Your Body*, he outlines how we can create new neural pathways by doing things differently. The more often we think the new thought, the stronger the pathway becomes.

So if you have a habit of thinking negatively, the fixed mindset would say, "It's just the way I am". If you adhere to David's theory, every time you think something negative, stop, take a breath, and create a more positive thought consciously. Every time you do this you will fire that new neural pathway and strengthen it.

Eventually, with repeated action, the new pathway will be the one that fires and the old, negative one will be reabsorbed by the brain. Isn't that marvellous?

After the stroke I had no feeling in my left hand and no strength in my arm, as well as other numbness down my side and on my face. I'll be honest, when I spoke to the neurologist I was scared. I cried, my mum cried, and then I went home and sat in the living room with the blinds shut. When Phil got home, I simply said, "I'm done." You see after my Lundy trip, I thought I had a decompression injury and they usually get better after treatment and a bit of time. I received fourteen hours of recompression therapy at the time and it had been six months, so I was expecting a full recovery by now. When the neurologist said "stroke", that sounded permanent.

So I sat in the dark for three days and people fed me

and brought me cups of tea (maybe that's why I prefer coffee these days?) and there was talk of closing my business.

On day three, after lots of sleep and feeling sorry for myself, I had a realisation.

I had A levels in Anatomy and Physiology, I knew how the body worked. Through my holistic therapy practice I had worked with two lovely ladies who had recovered from cancer. They had received chemotherapy, but said that Reiki had given them the strength to be positive and had reduced their symptoms.

Through reading David's books, I knew that every cell in the body rejuvenates, so in a seven year period we have a totally different body. It's only through muscle memory that our eyes remain short sighted, for example. All of the studying and personal development I had done had lead me to this moment; the strong and shouting thought that this was NOT going to be my reality.

If you want to read the whole story, I wrote it in *Rescued by The Coastguard*.

The short version is that when Phil came home that night I said, "I am going to get better and I'm going to dive again." His answer was, "Cool."

I didn't know how yet, but in that moment I changed my mindset and step by step, the answer pieced itself together. You see, if I could dive that meant I needed to be fit. My blood pressure needed to be normal, rather than the 203/125 it had been of late – a tad worrying after already suffering one stroke.

Three years later as I dived HMS Thistlegorm in the Red Sea, it wasn't my mask leaking that made my eyes salty, it was the tears of pure joy as I realised I had done it. I was completely recovered, full feeling in my whole body and blood pressure controlled; mission accomplished.

Since then, I've quartered the blood pressure medication I need, mostly corrected my eyesight, got my arthritis under control and all sorts of other wonders, but it all started with the assumption that there could be a better way, and an 'open and curious' attitude to giving it a try.

Mantras

I love a good mantra! A mantra is a positive statement around a chosen subject that, when repeated often can give a different experience.

Think of something that really grinds your gears –

and flip it.

You could start by reading the actual book *Flip It*, by Michael Heppell. This is one of the books that changed my life and how I think.

No money?

"I create my own economy and I attract money effortlessly."

No time?

"I always create time for the important things."

Want to be fitter?

"I love that my body supports me in everything I do."

Need something generic?

"I am safe, I am well, I trust myself."

You have to *do* something

Whether it's your reticular activating system, the energy of The Universe, your thought process, mantras… you have to DO something. You need to make a start. Even if you don't initially believe that something will work, you need to give it some energy.

Break your big vision down into smaller goals, then a list of actions that you can do every day.

Start acting as if things are different and watch for

the smallest of signs that it's working. If it doesn't? Then you will know. If it does? Life becomes a thrilling adventure of possibility!

So what will your vision be? It can be as simple or as complex as you like. You can focus on one thing or have a list! When you start with an idea, expand it. We usually start with what we have plus around 10% when budgeting, but what if life could be filled with 'big hairy audacious goals' as Jack Canfield suggests. Daily 'pinch me' moments that create a massive smile.

I'm writing this book mostly from beautiful campsites around Provence, France. I am doing some work, and of course writing, in between visiting gorgeous villages and seaside vistas. We're away for four weeks and I can, with confidence, work from anywhere. Remember that vision I set off in 2012? It's now a wonderfully delicious reality.

Dreams do come true. What would you wish for if you knew you couldn't fail?

NICKY'S TIPS TO SAVE YOURSELF
TIP SEVEN

Have you discovered your bounce?

"It's easy to be peaceful when you are on a mountain top eating berries, but if you can smile in a supermarket on a Saturday morning you have truly discovered your bounce."

Made up by me during a Keynote talk.

CHAPTER SIX
YOUR WELLBEING TOOLKIT

So much has been written about wellbeing in recent years, with sections on breakfast news, articles in every magazine and lots of celebrities sharing their own wellbeing secrets. To be honest, I love it.

Until every last person on the planet is happy and healthy there will always be room for more content, and in my view, it should be collaboration over competition anyway. We all have our unique way of sharing how we help and every person will find their own route to wellbeing – remember what I said about it being a personal recipe?

I don't see people saying there are too many applicants to MasterChef!

After the stroke I continued my practice at The Witches Brew, to give tarot readings and holistic therapies, but I felt there may be more ways to help. When someone had a reading with me, I would share inspiration around what was possible for them, but I knew generally people lacked the energy to make that dream a reality.

Some people would land on my couch for treatment and afterwards I would give them lots of tips for self-care between treatments. So many people just wanted to come back to me – they were too busy to do much in between.

As 2012 came to a close, I sold The Witches Brew and took a small therapy space in Keynsham. I was still questioning how I could help people more. By Spring 2013 I had written a six-part mentoring programme and started Discover Your Bounce; but I had no idea whether this could really help anyone.

I was networking regularly and so asked for guinea pigs to test my new programme. I worked with four people; two men and two women who each had six sessions over twelve weeks. I felt like weekly sessions didn't give people long enough to try something new, but once a month may mean losing focus.

Those first four clients had amazing successes; reducing anxiety, getting energy back after grief, getting inspired once more by life and business, and so I knew that The Bounce Programme worked. I was delighted to hear that my hunch was correct; people needed more.

The programme is a mix of self-awareness, empowerment and learning how the brain and body functions. There is a spiritual element there too, working with the chakras to boost energy and create balance and also working to create a strong vision.

Over the years I have seen people become resilient, energised, inspire, happier…*unfuckwithable*! It's a process, it's easy to follow and it works.

In 2017 I asked Sharon into the business as a non-executive director. I knew I needed some guidance to expand and grow the business; I had created several startups, but I felt DYB was a teenager that needed direction to grow into adulthood. The first thing Sharon did was to invite Laura, our then marketing director, and I over to France for a week of planning. It was here that I learned how to be an entrepreneur rather than replace my job with a business that owned me. I had always followed the nine-to-five, worked hard – too hard at times – and in doing so limited how our business could be. In that week we brunched by the pool and visualised with coloured pens and big pieces of paper, we discussed our vision and the details walking to and from restaurants, and a new vision for Discover Your Bounce sprung to life.

At the end of that year Laura pursued another exciting vision, and Sharon decided she didn't much like to word 'non' in her title.

We expanded Discover Your Bounce by creating a corporate workshop series and added a Leadership Development Programme too. Shortly after I had published *Rescued by The Coastguard,* we published one of my lovely mentoring clients Lynn's book and Discover Your Bounce Publishing was born.

My point is that wellbeing isn't just mental health. Wellbeing isn't ever just a basket of fruit in the kitchen and half-price gym membership for your employees. Although in 2017 that was the standard answer when we asked organisations about their wellbeing initiatives. Our early clients were banks and large organisations, but we were still labelled 'hippy'. Two people I respected at the time told me that, 'there is no place in the workplace for wellbeing'. My respect went at that point and of course the rest is history; post Covid the word wellbeing is used in most organisations.

We have created a wellbeing philosophy that has four elements:

Mind   Spirit

Body   Vision

Before I expand on mind, body and spirit now, have a think about what wellbeing means to you. How do you currently incorporate wellbeing activities into your life? As you read on, think about how easy it could be to include a few more activities.

Mind

Our mental health is on a sliding scale and can fluctuate depending on our energy levels, life's happenings, workload, family responsibilities, etc., as well as our own health and a myriad of other external factors. Wherever your mental health is today on a scale of one to ten is your current reality. Your emotions are your mental health compass; so think about how you have felt in recent weeks.

We are allowed to feel all of our emotions, where you are is valid and you shouldn't need to be 'fine' all the time. In fact, I've heard it said that 'FINE stands for fucked up, insecure, neurotic and exhausted'… I hope that made you smile!

Our brain is designed to keep us safe and has not evolved since the time of cave-dwelling. Our amygdala is constantly looking for threats and our hippocampus is constantly assessing whether that threat is valid. If we feel we are in danger, our adrenaline and cortisol levels rise in readiness to fight or flee – very useful when threats included sabre toothed tigers! But, in our modern world the 'threat' could be an email or a car cutting you off in traffic, but the reaction is the same. To 'use up' this stress response we need to get moving, so if something is stressing you, get your trainers on and go for a walk, or dance around the kitchen.

To stay calm we need to stay present and produce our feel good hormones: serotonin, dopamine, oxytocin and endorphins. I have come up with some suggestions of mind 'remedies' as ways to do this.

Our other two stress responses are freeze and faun. Freeze is literally that, we feel incapable of movement or thought. In times of stress according to David Hamilton, we lose sixty percent of our brain's ability to function as we are using the 'crocodile', or 'chimp' brain; the oldest part of our brain.

When we can move or distance ourselves from the perceived threat, we engage our pre-frontal cortex, the part of our brain that creates inspiration or critical thought.

The faun response is a trauma response. I've invited a wonderful person in to talk more on trauma in chapter eight. But our faun response is to people-please. Being genuinely nice is one thing, but doing what someone else wants because in the past we have had a dangerous reaction to saying 'no' is not. If we have been taught that to have an opinion or make up our own mind is not safe, then we will faun. I know this is how I responded for years. When I started to heal this behaviour I lost several friends. Perhaps they weren't friends, or perhaps they were attracted to the person I was within that trauma response. Either way, I wish them well.

Mind Remedies
Mindfulness
Breathe in for four and out for six three times and you will feel more present. Mindfulness is the art of staying mentally present for a period of time. When we can switch from stressful *thinking* to mindful *being* we encourage and build neuroplasticity; the brain's elasticity, a brain workout if you like. This enables us, in times of crisis, to regain our pre-frontal cortex thinking rather than being unable to think. We may ruminate about the past or stress about the future, but this present moment is the only one we can change.

Meditation

Meditation is a wonderful workout for the mind, body and spirit. I used to think that to meditate effectively I needed to sit still, without a thought and without moving for at least an hour. With an ADHD busy brain that did not go well! Thankfully I met some wonderful people that showed me different ways, and today we have amazing apps that can help us too.

Walking rhythmically is meditating. Washing up can be meditating. I have found my meditation to be in the swimming pool and at a dance class. The trick with meditation is not to react to thoughts; they will fly by and try to attract your attention. If you can just let them drift past, eventually, they will slow and you will probably ignore them completely.

Being honest here, I don't meditate all the time, nor do I do mindfulness practices consciously every day. In times of stress, or if I know I've got a busy time coming up, then I will do both a lot.

Breathing

You are alive, therefore you are breathing.

What if you chose to breathe consciously, deliberately, slowly? What if you could train your lungs to expand? What if you could get into sound sleep after the most stressful day, just by breathing?

You can!

We use a fraction of our lungs in day-to-day life, but they are enormous! Try to breathe in for the count of six, hold that count for six, breathe out for six and then – important bit – hold the out breath for the count of six. Repeat this three times, and you will have relaxed your body and oxygenated your brain. Perhaps your shoulders, jaw and tongue will have relaxed too. Do this repeatedly and over time your blood pressure will reduce, your lymph will flow better, and your body will detox. This can also help digest your food better. I had acid reflux for years, I don't now.

Nature

It is said that the ancient Greeks lived in fields. As they got more sophisticated they built massive, concrete cities and palaces for the gentry. Then the rich people indulged in trips out to the country to 'be' in nature - interesting, huh?

We are organic beings, and we crave natural environments. Ever had a problem you were trying to solve for ages and then suddenly, on holiday you had that 'aha' moment? We relax in nature, so maybe find some green spaces to hang out in. I'm writing most of this book in campsites around France, surround by trees and fields, it's a wonderful way to get creative.

Biophilia is something I have learned more about, and it really speaks to me. Psychology Today sums it up perfectly:

Biophilia, which literally translates to "love of life," is the idea that this fascination and communion with nature stem from an innate, biologically-driven need to interact with other forms of life such as animals and plants.

The more time I spend in nature, the less I worry about the small stuff.

Body

Our body is our vehicle that gets us from one place to the next, but sometimes we give our vehicle more attention. You wouldn't expect to get in your car and drive from Cornwall to Scotland without putting some fuel in or topping up the water but I know, myself included, at times we expect our body to just function without attention.

What does good physical health mean to you? Is it energy, flexibility, longevity… or just being able to get up and move in the morning?

Your vision will differ from someone else's, but it's good to stop and think about what you want from your body. In recent years after turning fifty I'm thinking more and more about positive aging, to continue to be fit and flexible; something I didn't give much thought to in my thirties.

TV and the media drip-feed subtle messages around what our body should be like. If you watch adverts, they tell us to eat and shop for food all the time. If you read magazines, they give us the image of the 'perfect' slim, tanned, flawless-skinned body. Mostly I pre-record the programmes I want to see and skip adverts, but when I occasionally do tune in – wow! I would be eternally hungry and never satisfied!

Physical health can come down to the basics; are you hydrated, fueled, well rested and physically active?

Body Remedies

Hydration

It's easy to check if you are hydrated – when you pee, is it the colour of champagne? Any darker and you probably need some more water. The guidance is two litres of water per day, but everyone is different, so use the pee test as a guide.

Nutrition

There is so much information available online about nutrition that I think most of us know what we should eat, but perhaps we are too busy to plan or too overwhelmed to make changes.

Some tips I've learned from dieticians:

If you make a fist, this is the amount of protein you should have in a meal. Carbohydrates should cover the palm of your hand. Fruit and vegetables – we should consume around thirty portions of fruit and vegetables in a week, the more varied and seasonable the better. In general, our food should be as unprocessed as possible. Shopping at markets, or around the edges of a supermarket should help with this; the 'beige' aisles are in the middle, usually with BOGOF offers and big labels to tempt us! Some is okay, lots is generally not advised.

Sleep

Sleep expert Dr Tara Swart recommends we have eight hours and fifteen minutes of sleep every night, lying on our side so that the glymphatic system can cleanse our brain of debris. On average, post-menopause, I get nine hours of sleep per night, but it hasn't always been this way and I know around half of the UK population struggle to sleep.

On our podcast, the My Wellbeing Show, we interviewed sleep expert Giles Watkins about how to have better sleep, and we frequently run free workshops on the topic as we know how important it is to your mental health, physical health and mood. One night of disturbed sleep can mean your mood drops significantly.

Activity

As a nation, our activity levels are falling each year and inactivity is linked to many physical conditions. You don't need to run a marathon or sweat it out in the gym - a gentle walk or some gardening also counts.

When I returned to ballet after a thirty-five year hiatus, I could hardly complete the class. Most of my classmates would then go straight into an hour of Dancefit (Zumba) and I was stunned. There was no way I could do that in my drippy, lobster-faced state!

Soon I was in the swing of ballet classes and decided to give Dancefit a try. At first, I struggled and had to step half of it, but now it's my Friday morning piece of heaven. No matter what else is going on in my life, through health scares and family heartache, when that music starts I'm in my happy place, with my 'Ballet Girls' - a group of ladies that I adore.

The guidelines suggest one hundred and fifty minutes of activity per week but start with five minutes of something you love and see how you feel. From tiny acorns, mighty oaks grow.

Extra Tips

There are some great apps to track your sleep and your activity, and using them can be a great way of noticing your progress.

Take on a charity challenge. I would not run for a bus, but recently ran a 10k! Why? It was for a fantastic charity. I had help from my friend Kelly who ran with me (love you!) and my brother Darren who had run half marathons previously. I really struggled to start with, but finished the race ten minutes earlier than my target time and really did enjoy some - not all - of our runs. Whether it's a run, a walk, a hula hooping session or skipping challenge, the point is it's a win/win and you are more likely to stay the course.

Spirit

The elements of spirit can be hard to quantify, but I think of our spirit as the thing that animates us, or makes us appear 'larger than life'. We talk about being 'in high spirits' and encourage with, 'that's the spirit!'

At Discover Your Bounce we talk about the elements of spirit being:

Happiness
Emotional Intelligence
Purpose
Community

Happiness

There are two types of happiness; extrinsic and intrinsic. Extrinsic happiness, as Wendy Brumwell talks about in her book, *A Successful State of Mind*, is happiness brought about by something external; a thing or an event. This kind of happiness can be fleeting and relies on something outside of our control. We can forever be chasing the next big thing and tell ourselves that 'I'll be happy when' rather than choosing to be happy first, with the thing being the icing on the cake.

Intrinsic happiness is simply happiness within. I think of it as a gentler experience; peace, contentment, a feeling of abundance and ease. Inner happiness brings wisdom, as we can think clearly and make our best decisions. It can't be taken away by another and doesn't rely on having things.

Sharon had a wonderful friend called Lisa, who had many challenges in her life before she died of complications from Osteogenesis imperfecta. During her illness, Sharon and Lisa had many laughter-filled moments and made the best of every experience. When it was her time, Lisa asked Sharon, "What makes you happy?" It had a massive impact on Sharon, and I would love to carry on Lisa's legacy by asking you to ponder on this very thing.

Emotional Intelligence

EQ - emotional quotient, or emotional intelligence enables us to have better relationships with others, as well as a better understanding of ourselves. We can identify what pushes our buttons and learn to respond differently. This enables us to be fearless and *unfuckwithable* as we learn skills to navigate the most delicate of scenarios.

I know many physically strong, intellectual people that shy away from a tricky conversation for fear of saying the wrong thing. I would encourage you to study this topic, or simply be open and curious around your relationships. When someone says something that perhaps you disagree with, know that in this moment this is absolutely their truth. From what they know and how they experience life, this is the conclusion they have come to.

You many need to give yourself some time to process the situation, you may need to ask a few questions to clarify what that person actually said; I know in high stress situations I can miss vital elements of what was said. You may need to agree to disagree.

I'm currently learning about Transactional Analysis from a book called *I'm OK, You're OK* by Thomas A Harris. We can always learn how to deepen and understand our relationships.

Of course, there are some relationships where your views are so different that continuing with the relationship is impossible and that's okay. I have a measure when someone has an opinion of me, I ask myself whether my mum would be okay with my actions or words, and if so, I let it go. It's taken me years to get to this point, but now I quite like me!

Purpose

I love Ikigai, the Japanese philosophy of purpose. 'Iki' means to live and 'gai' means reason. By asking what you love, what you can get paid for, what you are good at and what the world needs you can get to your Ikigai, or purpose – the thing makes you, *you*.

Your Ikigai may be made up of work and hobbies, rather than a whole solution in one place, but it's a nice way of getting to the root of meaning in your life.

Community

In this modern online age of delivery apps and virtual working, you need never leave your house. I believe that most of us yearn for some kind of human connection. It can be daunting to find a new community, but read on for some suggestions.

Spirit Remedies

When we are busy, we lose touch with what is important to us, and get lost in our to do lists and calendar appointments. It's usually during big life challenges and upheavals that we question, perhaps for the first time, what's important in our life.

Take an afternoon out somewhere beautiful, with a pretty notepad and ask yourself, what makes you truly happy. Aim for that intrinsic happiness, with a dash of the extrinsic too, a mix of contentment and fun.

Start somewhere. You don't need to get all of the elements in place immediately but start with a small thing and work up from there. Or dive right into a massive challenge if you like – that's the beauty of your life, you get to live it your way!

Find your communities. It could be a dance class, a singing group, a local green initiative. You could volunteer at a charity, or join The Ramblers. Spend time with people that have similar interests, or go for something completely new.

Take some time to think about your purpose and what gives your life meaning. Celebrate who you are and what you are passionate about.

And finally…

The best way to improve your wellbeing is to create a life you don't need to run away from. We used to talk a lot about 'stress management' but how about 'stress elimination'? When we do our own inner work, create supportive, loving relationships, choose a career or business that doesn't feel like work and spend time nurturing ourselves, life can feel wonderful.

Of course, we can't get from a place of suffering to a place of ecstasy in one easy step. We have to tune in to our inner voice, to get clear, to say yes and no to the right things and people. We need to spot when an opportunity for a quantum leap comes our way. I feel that the stroke experience was just that – would I have chosen it? Of course not, but it was an opportunity to make some big changes and learn some important lessons.

If you find yourself in a place you don't want to be, first be gentle. Then my hope is that you can use elements from this book, in no particular order, to make some gradual changes.

In line with the theme for this book, no workplace wellbeing scheme, or gym membership, or craze on TikTok is going to dramatically improve your wellbeing; you will. We all need to take personal responsibility for our own health and wellbeing.

Can a craze inspire you? Hell, yeah! Should your workplace support your wellbeing? Abso-bloody-lutely!

Is it inspiring to have somewhere you can go and get fit with a bunch of people that have a shared passion? Of course. But doing your own research into what suits you and creating a plan that you will enjoy will mean you are more likely to get started. Having a purpose or vision, a way of motivating yourself and a way to sustain yourself energetically will ensure that you stick to your plan.

Go back to your notes about what wellbeing means to you. Write four columns: mind, body, spirit and vision. Make notes on what you would love to do around these elements of your own wellbeing. In chapter ten we are going to look at your vision again, and these notes can be a part of that.

Sidenote:

The My Wellbeing Show podcast and our *Discover Your Bounce Community* on Facebook are full of inspiration on wellbeing, and the *Love Your Life* series of books provides practical tips and a journal where you can track your progress. For details head to the back of the book.

NICKY'S TIPS TO SAVE YOURSELF
TIP EIGHT

Feeling safe

If you are feeling anxious, are going to a new place or have a big meeting ahead, imagine a bubble of pure white light surrounding you. You can do this in the shower, in the car or at any point during any day – as you breathe imagine breathing in white light and then breathing it out into a protective bubble around you.

(Thanks Vicky Chidgey for remembering this one!)

CHAPTER SEVEN
TALKING ALL THINGS WOO!

Before we dive into your personal woo toolkit, let me tell you a story…

As a child I think I was very open to the spirit world, and working with several shamans over the years I don't think I was fully ready to be here. I took a very long time to be born, and was born not breathing so I was immediately wheeled off to the special care unit. My poor mum and dad didn't know whether I was alive for eight hours, until my lovely nan went to find me.

As a baby and child, I would scream if put onto grass or sand, anything 'of the earth' freaked me out completely. As a four-year-old I wouldn't take both feet off of the ground at the same time, perhaps I was scared that if I left the earth I wouldn't come back. I clearly remember a premonition dream I had as a four-year-old but then I went to school, started ballet - which became my absolute passion - and I think I plugged into the 'matrix' of this three-dimensional world.

As a teenager I was obsessed with all things spooky. I played with a Ouija board (only once as the results were too accurate!), I avidly read my stars, and as I grew into adulthood I regularly had tarot readings, palm readings, aura photos… anything esoteric and I was there.

Did I class myself as spiritual? Not at all. I got married, bought a house, had babies and played housewife. It was only when Kassi went to school that I had time to really think about myself, and to my delight one of the mums in Kassi's class read tarot. Maria had gone to the same senior school as me and I had gone to primary school with her brother, Marcus.

As I sat in her living room, before she had turned over a single card, she looked me dead in the eye and asked, "Why are you here? You are a Psychic Medium and can read your own cards." I replied that I couldn't, I was working in a bank and training to be an accountant, to which she gave me the most life changing reply. "That's what you do. It's not who you are."

My reading was all about finding myself and getting strong, which I took to mean physically, as I was suffering with horrendous gynaecological issues and had a hysterectomy two years later. It turned out her meaning went much deeper than that. Over several months I studied with Maria, unlocked my psychic and mediumship skills and really tuned into who I was, mentally, physically and spiritually.

I wrote *Tabby Turns the Tables* as a fictional book, but if you have read this far into my book you deserve to know a secret; Tabby's journey is my actual journey. Everything I wrote as a fantastical fiction story is absolutely true - if not way more weird! I had been born a Church of England Christian, but had never really *felt* like a Christian. I felt like everyone else had the memo and I did not.

Maria lent me a book, *A Witch Alone* by Marian Green and it absolutely changed my life. Everything she described as being Pagan, I naturally did. It turned out that the meditations I wrote were in tune with the moon cycles too. I devoured that book with delight and read many more just to prove to myself that this was a thing for me.

Over the years I have studied with Shamans and Druids, the Dobunni Grove of Druids have a special place in my heart as they welcomed me in and helped me with so many questions! That's what I love about Paganism, you can question everything and find your own way. The Witches' Rede states, "If it harms none, do as you will." I have read tarot for The Guardian recruitment fair, I have read for foreign royals, I have been a platform medium and served many churches. I teach tarot and psychic development, as well as Reiki and other energy healing techniques.

Once I told my mum about my journey, she shed light on my ancestors. Both my great grandmothers had been spiritual. My mum's nan read tea leaves and my dad's gran was a herbalist and medium. Why had I not been told this before? Perhaps I had never asked!

My coffee shop, The Witches Brew was an homage to the strong women that went before me. My interpretation of witch was Woman In Total Charge of Herself and my coffee shop was bright and welcoming. We did have a spiritual circle that was held monthly and we sold crystals, but generally we were just a supportive coffee shop and holistic therapy centre, nothing more.

One day while I was in the shop, Marian Green visited for a coffee. She had heard of my shop and got the bus to say Hi. My idol, this wonderful lady that had changed my life, visited my shop! I took this as a very good omen and didn't stop smiling for days.

My spiritual journey has taken me to amazing places, on this planet and in the esoteric world. It's important to say here I don't expect you to follow my path, or even believe what I believe. I have seen so many things for myself that I'm convinced of the reality I have come to know. If you read quantum theory then my reality is happening because I am observing it, and so you will experience your own, simply because you are the observer. My invitation to you is to read, experiment and use the tools that feel right in your heart. Nothing need make logical sense, but in your gut and heart it should *feel* natural.

Okay for this next bit strap yourself in, we're going to go FULL WOO WOO!

Over the years I have delved into the science of wellbeing, the psychology of happiness and the intelligence of coaching and EQ. No matter how much science I learn, I still combine all my spiritual teachings into my work. I like to think that my roots were all woo woo, and now with a bit of science in the mix I'm just woo. A woo woo is not just a cocktail - it's a place, between worlds, where you can create big personal development leaps and massively shift how you feel about yourself and the world around you. I have made quantum leaps in my life by being open to working with different energies. I've changed my life and health beyond everything I thought possible, and so can you.

So here we go, the full Woo Toolkit, from my heart and mind to yours…

First, let's talk about the dimensions

As we have come to know, everything is made up of molecules; we are all a collection of shimmering particles and I've always struggled with that concept, seeing everyone and everything as solid. However, during Reiki sessions, in meditation, and through studying to see auras I have had moments of seeing people in this way.

During your spiritual journey you may hear people talking about different dimensions. We can look at a drawing on paper and see this as 2D and of course we see our everyday world in 3D. In 3D it's a bit like having a fixed mindset, we think the world is as we see it and we are unable to create change. 3D is quite a heavy energy, it's where we see and feel fear.

As we learn and grow, we can shift our experiences into 4D, this is the level of infinite possibility. We access this fourth dimension through meditation, music, art, yoga… any activity where we can dissolve our fear, forget the constraints of time and place and just be as an energetic being. Have you ever had a massage and felt that 'not asleep, not awake' feeling of ease and peace? This is 4D. When we are in flow with the Law of Attraction, this is also the fourth dimension.

It's been said that as we have moved into the Age of Aquarius, we are more able to create a 5D world. This is where we can create, and change, our reality by changing our energy. In 5D we experience and give unconditional love. We let go of worry and power and experience a blissful state of heaven on earth. The fifth dimension may need a shift in how we approach life, like giving thanks for the gas bill as it allows us to keep warm.

This 5D state is available to us all, but not everyone would believe in it or choose it. The journey does require us to deal with our traumas, let go of our limiting beliefs and stay present, grounded and centred.

No matter how many years you have been working on this, the reality is that you move between third, fourth and fifth dimensions due to living in our current reality. You can meditate and feel light, eat or drink too much and feel heavy. Go for a massage and feel light, receive a stressful email and it's straight back to heavy.

I do believe that the work is worth it though; the lows aren't as low and don't last as long, our abilities get sharper and we can spot some of the challenges before they reel us in. Once you have experienced the blissful states that are possible, it's like muscle memory – it's easier to get back to peaceful.

Again, I introduce this here as a concept, I invite you to notice how you feel when you go about your day. Listen to a meditation and notice if your energy shifts. If you find yourself worried or fearful, try to get out in nature and do a breathing exercise and see if you can change your state.

Next, let's journey into the chakras

After the birth of my second child, my health took a real turn for the worse. Looking back, I think that as my world collapsed, my body did too. Kassi was nearly 9lbs born and five weeks late - perhaps not the best combination although I will forgive them as they spent their days smiling! I didn't know, but I had a severe womb prolapse that went undiagnosed for six years, resulting in me having a hysterectomy at twenty-nine.

This meant daily pain, reduced mobility, regular anaemia, and three weeks each month of really heavy bleeding. My GP was sympathetic, but after a consultation when an aging, pompous consultant wrote that, "this stressed-out housewife needs to learn to go home and calm down," he couldn't really do much to help except prescribe painkillers that didn't work. At that time, I was run down, depressed and switched off, so I didn't really have the energy to advocate for myself.

One day I had a tarot reading from a lovely lady called Sue. She could see from how I moved that I was in a lot of pain and asked if I had heard of the chakras; I had not. She drew me a little diagram of a stick man, got Kassi's crayons and drew circles, in rainbow colours at various points on the body. She taught me a simple way of visualising each chakra, seeing it as a healthy, vibrant colour, spinning in a clockwise and even fashion. She said this would help with my pain and to be honest, I did not for a second believe her. But I was curious, she sounded so convinced.

That night as I lay in bed with my stomach burning in pain, I closed my eyes and imagined a red disc at my abdomen. In my head I lifted it up until it was in front of my eyes – seeing it in my mind's eye. As I looked at it, I could see it was swollen, dark red, irregular and seemed angry. I imagined taking a jug and scooping some of the colour out. As I did so it regained a beautiful crimson colour. As I let it go it was spinning but really slowly, so with my next breath I imagined it speeding up, spinning in a level and easy way. Within minutes my pain had subsided enough so that I could sleep.

Wow!

Over the next few nights, I got better and better at seeing these discs, of balancing the colours and having much improved sleep. My daytime pain became manageable - during periods not so much - but it was so much better generally.

I then learned Reiki, or should I say Reiki found me?! On a holiday in Spain, I sat next to a lovely lady - also called Sue. It was her first solo holiday with her children, and she was a bit apprehensive. I gave her big smiles and gave her a rundown of the resort as we'd arrived a few days earlier. We sat together for a few days and got acquainted. She told me she was a Reiki master and in answer to my blank look told me what it was and how it worked – following the philosophy of Doctor Mikao Usui to direct universal life force through the body to help it to heal itself. I thought this sounded amazing and asked how you learn. She told me to find a Reiki master to attune me and, as we didn't live near one another she smiled and said, "If it's meant to be, you will find the right person."

During the years after my divorce, I saw Reiki in many places, but it was never the right time to take it further. Until one day, my fabulous friend and homeopath Mary told me she had a new partner and guess what? He was a Reiki master! She and I learned together, and they were amazing days.

Through this series of synchronicities and learning Reiki I was taught about the chakras in greater detail. Ancient traditions have been using this method as a system of healing for centuries and in this modern world it works just as well.

Chakras govern the mind, body, and spirit. It's a bit of a chicken and egg scenario; do we struggle because a chakra is out of alignment, or does the illness unbalance the chakra? Honestly, I don't know, but I have used chakras in my own meditations and within my holistic therapies for twenty years to great effect.

There are many books on the subject, but here is a quick run-down of the chakras and what they govern.

The Root Chakra

The root chakra is located at the base of the spine. It dictates how well we are grounded; it is our contact with ourselves and what we stand for as individuals. This chakra also takes care of our sexual desire and ability to survive. In the event of poor operation: Obesity, haemorrhoids, constipation, and sciatica.

The Navel (Sacral) Chakra

The navel chakra is located under the belly button and its primary function is procreation and sexuality. Another function of the Navel chakra is that is works as a centre of cleansing for the body. Blockage of this chakra can result in both relationship and menstruation problems.

The Solar Plexus Chakra

This chakra is located above the navel and the chakra is related to our self-esteem and image of ourselves. Because the chakra affects the nervous system as well as our blood circulation in the event of poor operation, the following can occur: diabetes, eating disorders, and low blood sugar.

The Heart Chakra

The heart chakra relates to self-love, love and compassion; it's thus related to trust, love and stronger feelings. Problems with and blockage of this chakra might cause a wide range of emotional disorders as: jealousy, pain, hate, grief and fear.

The Throat Chakra

This chakra controls everything related to our communication. When a person experiences communication problems it's highly probable that the throat chakra is blocked.

The Third Eye Chakra

The chakra called the third eye is located in the forehead, between the eyes. This chakra is about intuition and clairvoyance; more specifically it's about the spiritual development of the self. As a result, the chakra is linked to our brain and other physical parts such as the nose and eyes.

The Crown Chakra

In difference to the other chakras this one doesn't relate to a body organ. Instead, it's located at the top of the head. This chakra connects us to the universe and its energy, the energy from the universe comes into the body through the crown chakra.

Your Total Woo Kit

There are a few tools that it may be fun to work with, to help and to guide you in your spiritual development. On good days these will be fun to try but at times when you are feeling stuck, when challenges appear or when you are feeling under the weather, these tools can be your saviour.

Now I will add here that if your physical or mental health is suffering then you should consult a doctor. If you have financial worries you should see your financial advisor and it's always good to have a friend to chat things through with.

I have a feeling that you already know this, right?

Sometimes, we just need a bit of space to work things out for ourselves. Sometimes, we have a feeling about what we should do, but perhaps we're not totally sure or we're just not ready. Remember what I said about boosting your energy before a big project or life change? Your woo toolkit will be useful during these moments.

The beauty of always being able to save yourself is that when life gets going again, you are on your own perfect path. By boosting your own wellbeing and tuning into your innate wisdom, you are doing things your way. Sometimes when someone else saves us it can feel like a relief, but then we find ourselves in a situation that doesn't sit quite right.

Your Woo Toolkit will allow you some time and space for self-reflection, self-discovery and self-actualisation - that's a lot of self! And oh my goodness the feels when you have got to that new place are so sweet!

Here is what I would suggest for some retail therapy for the soul.

Sage or Palo Santo (Sacred Pine)
If you feel a bit sluggish, if the energy in your house feels flat, if you have been ill, had a row or been around someone challenging then 'smudging' is the perfect pick me up. Choose sage or pine, light it and then blow it out until it's just smoking. Carry an Abalone shell or side plate around with you to catch any bits and waft smoke (smudge) around yourself and your environment. As you do so imagine any heavy energy being replaced by

light. Perhaps see yourself smiling and happy, or set some intentions, like your house being a place of inspiration and happiness, your body being healthy and well, or your soul being peaceful and centred. When you are finished stub out the sage or pine, open a few windows and perhaps light a candle or incense.

Crystals

Crystals have a wonderful energy, and my house is full of them. I have crystal skulls, balls, palm stones, rough bits and animals. In my humble opinion you can never have enough crystals.

Each crystal has properties, and *The Crystal Bible* by Judy Hall is a great book to get started. You can research crystals and buy according to your research, but my suggestion would be to just see what ones you are drawn to. Once you have chosen, then look up the meaning and you will find that it's either perfect now, or in the very near future.

Carrying a crystal in your pocket or bra can give you confidence in an important meeting. They can reassure you on an anxious drive. They can help you to sleep or raise your vibration. I get mine from my friend Jemima due to her beautiful energy and careful buying, you can find her at *Jimbles Crystals* – www.crystals-online.co.uk.

Tarot and Oracle Cards

I pick a card most days, to check in with myself, to get some guidance or just because I can!

Tarot can take a bit more getting used to and I suggest doing some kind of psychic training, so that you are using your intuition as you read the cards rather than just reading from the book. There is nothing wrong with book meanings, but using intuition just enriches your reading.

Oracle cards are a great starting point. You can pick a card in the morning to influence your day, or choose a card or two when making decisions.

Maybe ask a few friends round and read for each other – I would just suggest if you are having a few drinks do this after – I never mix my spirits!

After doing any intention setting, smudging or card reading I always suggest eating and drinking something to bring you back down to earth.

Signs

As you get more in touch with yourself you will be more in tune with the world around you. At this point you may notice more signs, or perhaps this is already a thing for you. Seeing 11.11 everywhere you go, a robin appearing in strange places, noticing white feathers, or the same line from a song being in every shop.

In the years I've been with Phil he has noticed more and more the signs around us. Initially he would just laugh and call it coincidence, but so many specific things have happened he now totally believes in signs.

One day I was doing a tarot reading for a lady and saw that she would see a feather, as a sign that this reading was important for her, within the next few hours. Two hours later she rang to say that her mobile had stopped working on her drive home – and that there was a feather between the battery and the contact. I was really impressed by that one!

Signs should be specific and feel right to you. One magpie is a sign for me that I'm on the right track, a blackbird flying in front of my car is a sign to slow down as there is a car coming around a narrow bend. If you see something three times, head to Google and search for the spiritual meaning of that bird, number or animal – the answers may surprise you, or at least make you smile.

Ayni

I was introduced to the term Ayni by a very wise soul and I want to share it here. Ayni means, to be in right relationship, with other beings, Mother Earth (Pachamama) and the Universe.

"Today for you, tomorrow for me."

It's the energy of reciprocity, doing something for the good of another or the planet without agenda, but in doing so good deeds automatically come your way. I was told that when we live in Ayni, we are recognised as a part of nature, when we are angry or selfish, we are no longer recognised, and challenges can come our way.

I believe that if more people are connected to the spiritual energy of this planet there would be a lot more giving and a lot less taking. If you look into the eyes of another and see the spark of spirit, it becomes harder to hate. You can have more empathy, even if someone is doing something that feels wrong to you. Perhaps you can give them an extra minute, or take a breath to ponder on their journey. This does not excuse hurtful behaviour, but this could mean letting someone go in front of you, forgiving an emotional outburst, or at least allowing an apology.

Our planet is suffering and we are suffering. Before we can look at sustaining the planet we need to sustain ourselves and other humans. Happy people make good choices, they care and they want to preserve not destroy. Happy, spiritual people are kind, they step over ants and make long term, thought-through decisions rather than knee-jerk, short-term reactions.

If all the people in charge of our planet were connected spiritually and looked after their own wellbeing, I believe we would live in a very different world indeed.

NICKY'S TIPS TO SAVE YOURSELF
TIP NINE

Thank you for…

Having an attitude of gratitude is so good for our mind, body and spirit. If the cat's been sick, you've run out of coffee and the Wi-Fi is down and it's only 8am, start to list your gratitudes. Perhaps the sun is shining, or you have 4G, or you have a friend to support you…or it's a weekend. Find at least three things to be grateful for, really feel them and watch your physiology change to a positive state.

CHAPTER EIGHT
WHAT IS RESILIENCE ANYWAY?

The dictionary meaning states that resilience is:

The capacity to withstand or to recover quickly from difficulties; toughness.

And an alternative:

The ability of a substance or object to spring back into shape; elasticity.

The American Psychological Association gives us this interpretation:

Resilience is the process and outcome of successfully adapting to difficult or challenging life experiences, especially through mental, emotional, and behavioural flexibility and adjustment to external and internal demands.

Let's take these meanings one at a time.

To withstand or recover from difficulties and

toughness. It would be lovely if we didn't have tough times or difficulties from which we need to recover, but as my lovely friend Nick Elston says,

"Life is not a Disney movie where everything comes right in the end."

Sometimes life truly sucks and can keep dishing out the tough times again and again. It can feel like life will never be fun again. It's at this point that we may need to dig deep, tuck in and stay the course, no matter how dark it can feel.

Sometimes we can wade our way through the mire that is life, other times we need to give in, retreat, lick our wounds, pout a lot and then decide what to do next.

I have often questioned why hard times come along for the loveliest of people. When thinking about God, or a Universe that delivers the most magical of experiences, if such a power exists why do such atrocious and tragic situations also occur? I try not to watch the news, but when I do it's painful to witness some of the horrors happening on our planet.

I have no answers.

I have often questioned my own purpose, my raison d'être - why I was popped on this planet at this point in space and time. I have tried many things, experienced a lot and I have concluded that throughout my entire life I have wanted to help people. I'm always *that* person who has a wet wipe, a plaster or a tissue in my handbag. I'll spot when someone is struggling to open a door with a buggy or needs some extra change at the checkout. I cry at everything; when a toddler falls over or at the end of a movie and I used to think that made me weak.

It's only been through my forties and fifties that I no longer get embarrassed when I cry. I'm proud that I care, happy that I have a big heart… and I really do give the best hugs!

I was presenting a workshop on resilience at an organisation recently and a wonderful neurodivergent attendee said, "I feel like this is a silly question, but what actually is resilience anyway?" I love my fellow neuro-spicy brained people, as you can count on us to interrupt the status quo and question something that may seem obvious to most, or those that don't get it just won't ask.

Her question sparked a lovely discussion around generations who had experienced war, or heard tales from their grandparents of loss, fear and scarcity. How people in their 50s can remember the Falklands war and the miners' strike and perhaps have brought up their children to not suffer, or go without, or ponder their own mortality by trying to wrap them in safety. I know when the COVID-19 pandemic happened, I spoke to a lot of younger people about the terror they felt, the helplessness and the uncertainty around what was to come.

Resilience is something we cultivate through hard times. We will all have our own ways of coping and getting through challenges. Some people will prefer to be with others, some people will battle through alone. When the storm passes, we will be stronger and wiser, and perhaps good days will feel a bit sweeter as a result.

The second definition (the one about elasticity) is not really talking about resilient materials, but the ability to spring back into shape, or to be elastic. In our business we talk about *Bouncebackability* and I hope that this book has given you some tools and inspiration to work out your own way to bounce!

If you know you will bounce back, it's a great feeling. When tough times arrive you can be safe in the knowledge that you will be okay. I have had a year of tests, consultants, hospital visits and surgery. I've had a few health concerns that, although minor have been debilitating and I've needed to rest. I've also got a recent diagnosis of diverticulosis, that is a serious, lifelong condition which needs careful management. Of course, it was a shock (as well as really bloody painful!) and I have had some 'poor me' moments. But as with my experience of the stroke, I know I'll be okay. There may be tough times ahead, there are many adjustments, but I'm not going to waste precious planet time wishing it was different.

Perhaps this is what resilience is.

The third definition states:

… the process and outcome of successfully adapting to difficult or challenging life experiences… through mental, emotional, and behavioural flexibility and adjustment to external and internal demands.

When we reach a block in the road, we definitely need to stop. At this point I recommend a scream and shout, some chocolate and a good movie. I also recommend you immediately up your self-care and reduce your diary commitments.

Then plan your bounce back!

Flexibility is key, as is an open and curious growth

mindset to allow you to create something different. At times when I have thought I had lost something, in the long-run I have always gained something more valuable. I encourage you to be brave, to get support, to nurture and repair – and then to rise like a beautiful phoenix to heights you never thought possible.

I believe in you.

NICKY'S TIPS TO SAVE YOURSELF
TIP TEN

The money tap

Money can be a big energy drain, so if you are in need of more money imagine there is a huge tap that rains golden coins straight into your purse or bank account. All you need to do is turn on that tap, and then act as if money is effortlessly on its way to you.

(Another thank you to Michelle Armitage for reminding me of this one!)

CHAPTER NINE
MORE WORK TO DO!

By now if you've been reading along and making notes, you probably have a list of what to do, as well as areas where you are happy with what you already do. Life can be a constant refining process, where we try as we go. Some things work for us, others don't. But either way - we find out. If you never take a step or try anything for fear of getting it wrong, you may never make that breakthrough. Even when something fails, we learn.

The trick is to gradually stretch away from your comfort zone into a stretch zone, by changing one thing at a time. If we change everything all at once we can slip into a panic zone, where everything has changed and we have no recognisable landscape. This can feel too uncomfortable to sustain.

Today I got back on a bike and rode after a twenty-five year break. We're in a beautiful campsite nestled by a lake, in a tranquil forest. I could have said no to the bike for a hundred reasons and believe me, my amygdala was reminding me loudly that I could fall, that I have arthritis, that it's hot and I could get sunstroke. But, I did it anyway. Was it pretty? No! Did I whine a bit? Yes! I even exclaimed to Mr M that he 'left me to die' at one point (not my finest moment). Will I ache tomorrow? Oh yes! The point is though, I have a wonderful memory, we had a giggle and none of the things that I worried about happened (except perhaps the aching!).

However, there are times when we are doing all the things and still not making progress or we get so far and suffer a setback. I wanted to talk about some of the reasons that may be happening in this chapter.

Once again, I'm going to talk about doing what is right for you.

There will be times when you can battle through, have an inspirational moment and win the day. There will be other times when your chosen step will be too hard and I have no problem quitting when it's obvious that something is not going to work. When Phil took up flying a glider, I had one flight with an instructor and that was me done. I didn't hate it; I just knew it wasn't my thing.

There are times when you know something is right, it's just not the right time. Or you know it's the right time but you have yet to find the right thing. Life is a bit like trying to solve a puzzle and peel an onion at the same time. The puzzle pieces are the external places, people and events, while the onion is your emotional and physical learning. It can take a while to find all the pieces and slot them into place, and I have always said I'm only up for peeling one onion!

What can get in your way
Our own B.S.
I have had to call bullshit on my own thinking so many times, but when I am in the moment it feels so real and so loud. It's only when I step away or give myself time that I can come to the realisation I am getting in my own way.

Since the menopause, the ADHD has got much more pronounced and when I am stressed or trying something new, I can get really frustrated and vocal about how I feel. If I am overworked or overwhelmed, the world closes in, I can hear people breathing or chewing, the air seems to not have any oxygen in it and I want to run away.

When it first started happening it was distressing, but over time I have learnt to step away. To hand over the thing, to not say immediately what's on my mind or even to have a nap (any excuse for a nanny nap).

Your feelings are your feelings and they are always valid. Given time though, you may decide to give it another go in a different way or enlist the help of someone who has been there or knows you. It's true no one can save you, but of course someone can support you.

Ask yourself questions like:
>   Is this reminding me of a past stressful time?
>   Is this the right time to be doing this?
>   Am I with the right people to support me?
>   How badly do I want to do this?

Above all be gentle, the world can be a stressful and overwhelming place at times, and we can be very hard taskmasters to ourselves.

Other people's B.S.
People can be amazing and lovely, and people can be dicks. Amazing and lovely people can also unwittingly

discourage us in their quest to keep us safe. I know this firsthand. Years ago when a friend was going through a divorce I tried to 'save' her from the pain and heartache. I tried to do everything for her, tried to stand up for her to her ex-husband and in doing so made things worse. She lovingly told me to mind my own business, which stung a bit but was fair.

Going through her own divorce, through those tough times really gave her time to understand who she was. She found a level of grit and struck out for the life she really wanted. Watching her go through this (without helping), I was amazed at her determination and her ability to go through tough times with grace and dignity.

Sometimes challenges show us who we really are, but the opinions of others can cloud our minds. Of course, we can listen to others, but always find some quiet space to listen to your own heart and gut, to breathe and feel and hear your own whispering intuition.

Oh, and some people really are just dicks, and you should not listen to them!

Working through your own shadow

When I asked Maria years ago whether she was a white witch, she gave me an answer that shaped my own journey. She said that it would be very hard to completely white, or completely black. She said that life happened in the grey.

We can try to be a good person, we can do good deeds, meditation, be kind, give back… but we are allowed to have human moments where we say or do the wrong thing. In times when I'm feeling stroppy and full of rage, I can yell and swear and spit venom (usually at myself), but then something will happen to snap me out of it, and I'll burst out laughing.

Living in the grey

Our shadow self is the side we hide away, to protect ourselves, through past traumas, or because we are ashamed. When we are trying to do something new, or 'spiritually level up', that is usually the time when our shadow self demands to be heard. It can be an inner child moment, a past life echo, something from a past relationship… so much of our identity happens subconsciously. You may not know exactly what it is, but perhaps you just get a feeling that what is holding you back is energetic.

Past trauma

This is such an important topic that I have called in my amazing friend Teresa Ridley to share her thoughts and learnings with you. There is a lot of information shared here and it may feel quite heavy but I think it's important to understand how we may be living our life with unresolved trauma influencing our decisions. You may also work with someone, or have a loved one that is dealing with trauma, so it's really valuable to know what could be going on for them too.

INNER WORK & TRAUMA – WHY WE NEED TO HEAL TRAUMA AND HOW IT CAN HOLD US BACK!

BY TERESA RIDLEY

What is trauma?

Trauma is the physical and emotional response that happens within our bodies' nervous systems and can occur when we are exposed to an event that we perceive as overwhelmingly distressing, threatening or dangerous.

It can leave us feeling helpless, frightened,

horror-stricken, in shock or profoundly unsafe and surpass an individual's natural capacity to effectively process the event both mentally and emotionally and adapt to an overwhelming situation.

Trauma can stem from a wide range of events, including but not limited to: natural disasters, violent assault, physical assault, domestic or sexual abuse, a serious accident, witnessing violence, the death of a loved one, military combat, chronic illness, a medical procedure, bullying, or from prolonged stressors, such as childhood neglect, having lived in war a torn country and terrorism.

Two people can both experience the same traumatic event, but could present different physical, mental and emotional nervous system responses, as safety may mean something entirely different from one person to the next based from their pre-existing childhood perceptions of danger, experiences, attachments and protector parts. This will in turn will have a profound impact on the way the traumatic event is processed.

The aftermath of trauma can continue to echo through a person's psyche, impacting on both their cognitive and emotional function long after the actual event, often invading even the most private and guarded recesses of the mind.

Trauma can manifest as a profound reaction to an experience that encompass various forms of threat. Whether that's physical, emotional, or psychological in nature, it bears the potential to leave an intense and lasting impression on an individual's mental and emotional wellbeing, which has the ability to change the way they process, function, respond and interact with others, due to the heightened activation of their nervous system.

When faced with a traumatic event our brain and body's stress response system instinctively responds to protect us. This involves the activation of our 'fight, flight or freeze' responses, which is known as hyperarousal. These are our natural evolutionary protective responses designed to shield us from immediate danger and it's that primitive part of the brain that we develop first, which is responsible for controlling our basic functions such as, breathing, blinking, digestion and our fight-flight responses.

When the body's stress response system goes into

high gear, it releasees our stress hormones such as cortisol and adrenaline, which can lead to an increase in our heart rate, elevated blood pressure, our breathing can become rapid, we can experience muscle tension and our senses will be heightened.

All of these natural survival responses are key for surviving situations where a quick reaction is needed to confront or escape danger. However, hyperarousal can become problematic if it persists long after the threat of danger has disappeared, for example persistent feelings of anxiety, restlessness, difficulty sleeping and relaxing, leading to various long-term physical and psychological symptoms that will interfere with an individual's daily life, including the way we show up, behave, respond and interact with others both on a personal level and in the workplace.

Trauma can also manifest in physical symptoms such as headaches, stomach ache, muscle tension and other psychosomatic complaints. More than eighty percent of chronic illness like: diabetes, asthma, arthritis, epilepsy, chronic fatigue and high blood pressure are caused by stress.

Someone who has experienced trauma may also

undergo changes in their mood and behaviour, such as; withdrawing from social activities and avoiding interaction with others, they may have increased irritability, experience mood swings and start to engage in risky behaviours like: alcohol or substance abuse, gambling, eating disorders and self-harm. Risky behaviours can bring momentary relief and are used as a coping mechanism to avoid distressing feelings or emotions and as a way of self-numbing.

Many of us will experience some form of trauma at some stage in our life, it's not a one-size-fits-all concept. There is no one way to determine who will suffer trauma and who will not, because we have all walked and experienced very different paths.

Trauma by its very nature, leaves an imprint. While the physical effects can be immediate and visible, the psychological and emotional aftermath might remain obscured, buried deep within the survivor's psyche.

At the heart of all our responses lies the brain. When trauma strikes, the brain activates our defence mechanism, the amygdala, which is known as our internal smoke detector and is responsible for detecting undergo changes in their mood and detecting and alerting us to perceived threat or danger within our environment.

In contrast, the hippocampus, which helps us process memory can shrink, potentially affecting our ability to create memories. In addition, the prefrontal cortex, responsible for our rational thought and decision-making process might become impaired, making it challenging for survivors to respond calmly to subsequent stressors or triggers.

The altered brain chemistry can also lead to imbalances in our neurotransmitters affecting our mood, our behaviour and our stress responses. Over time these neurobiological changes can pave the way for mental health disorders like PTSD, anxiety and depression.

Trauma survivors may also experience some of the following psychological manifestations:

- Disruptive memories / or flashbacks
- Difficulty sleeping or nightmares
- Emotional numbness
- Intense feelings of guilt or shame
- Low self-worth

- Lack of trust
- Difficulty forming close personal relationships.
- Chronic anxiety
- Burnout
- Depression
- PTSD
- Hyperarousal
- Dissociation and emotional numbing (which serves as a defence mechanism allowing the individual to distance themselves from overwhelming emotions or memories).

After experiencing a traumatic event, the world is seen through very different eyes and our nervous system will have an altered perception of risk and safety. The ripple effect of trauma can touch every aspect of a survivor's life. This includes their relationships, both personal and professional, which can become strained due to heightened irritability, withdrawal and fear of intimacy. Work performance may also suffer due to a lack of concentration, or chronic fatigue resulting from sleep deprivation and anxiety. Even mundane everyday tasks can become insurmountable challenges that feel overwhelming.

This is why understanding trauma is crucial.

- It gives us the ability to recognise and understand how trauma can impact individuals both physically and psychologically, help individuals by offering the appropriate support, empathise and implement the right infrastructure within the workplace which is vital for fostering a sense of safety and trust in relationships.

- Leaders can be far more effective if they have a better understanding and are educated on how trauma impacts individuals, this will help their teams significantly by fostering a safe environment where individuals are able to communicate, feel comfortable sharing their experience and seek help without judgement or fear. Where they are seen, heard, validated, shown compassion, empathy and offered the right support. A trauma informed leader will have the power to empower others and reduce the stigma that surrounds mental health within the workplace.

- If untreated, trauma can lead to the development of mental health issues such as anxiety, depression and post-traumatic stress disorder (PTSD). Understanding trauma can facilitate early intervention, treatment and promote better mental health outcomes.

- A deeper understanding of trauma helps reduce the stigma surrounding mental health. People who have experienced trauma may be less likely to feel isolated and more inclined to seek help if they know they won't be judged or shamed but listened to with empathy, compassion and understanding.

- Learning about trauma can lead to personal growth and resilience. Individuals who understand trauma may develop better coping strategies and emotional regulation skills, contributing to their overall wellbeing.

- Understanding trauma is essential in creating safe spaces and environments in various settings, such as schools, workplaces and our communities. This involves implementing practices that promote emotional safety, transparency, open communication, validation and support for all individuals, where healing can be nurtured, trust can be fortified and hope is rekindled.

- Practicing self-care is an integral part of an individual's road to processing what they have experienced, healing and their recovery.

Whilst trauma is a fact of life, it doesn't however, have to be a life sentence.

About Teresa

Teresa is passionate about mental health, having experienced her own personal trauma journey. This has led her to study a CPI Level 7 qualification to become a Somatic Trauma Informed Coach and Leader, which is also ICF & CPD accredited. Once fully qualified, Teresa will be looking to help others who have been on their own trauma journey as well as educate business leaders to have a better

> understanding of how they can implement safe working environments for their staff.
>
> "Somatic is the study and understanding of the internal physical and mental reactions and its impact our nervous system and body experiences based on our perception of danger from our past childhood core wounds".
>
> Teresa is in the process of setting up **The Petals Transformation Programme (Plant, Encourage, Transform, Awaken, Learn, Strength)** which will be up and running next year.
>
> If you would be interesting in finding out how Teresa can help you, please email: teresa@petalsprogramme.co.uk

It's very hard working all these things out for yourself; we can be too close to the situation to get to its root. I would say first try meditating, or find a beautiful place and sit with your journal. Then maybe turn over a few cards and see if all becomes clear. This can be a really effective way of working through your stuff.

If, however, you are still struggling, the temptation may be to just accept this is the way you are. This may keep you stuck. There are the most amazing therapists and healers in this world and I have had the pleasure - or pain - of working with some amazing people (doing the work can be hard!). Whether it's; Hypnotherapy, Regression or Timeline Therapy, Homeopathy, Kinesiology, Shamanic Healing, Reiki, Shiatsu, Bach Flower Remedies, Trauma Therapy, Counselling - or a hundred other modalities that I have yet to try - there is usually a way to work through and let go of the energy that is waiting to be released.

I sometimes think life is like an adventure game, it's only when we reach certain levels that we unlock a challenge. Solving the puzzle allows us to move to the next level. It can indeed be hard but it is usually worth it.

Mirrors

Have you ever met someone that has enraged you instantly? Or found someone close to you exhibiting behaviour that pushes all of your buttons?

Life can hold up a mirror to the part of us that needs healing.

Years ago, when all of our children lived at home, I found my stepson's behaviour enraging. He would look after himself, get up in the morning and do whatever he pleased. I mentioned this to Phil, who didn't seem bothered, and this was the clue that perhaps it was my issue not his. I sat for a while to contemplate the energy behind this and realised that I didn't have a minute to myself. With school runs, working, keeping a house going for six of us there was always so much to do. I realised his behaviour wasn't the reason for my rage: I was jealous. I started to give myself a bit more 'free time' and less of a 'hard time' and his behaviour no longer bothered me.

If you find that something is pushing your buttons it can be useful to give yourself time. Using emotional intelligence techniques, try to describe how you feel. Ask yourself if this situation is a reminder of a past experience or if you are tired, run down, or not feeling confident in yourself. Ask yourself if you are ready to diffuse the energy of this situation, or do you need to talk it through with a friend or professional?

I have found a great visualisation to use when people and their behaviour can feel challenging. Imagine gifting them flowers, or giving them a hug. If this feels too hard; don't. We don't need to get on with everyone, something I have found quite liberating.

We can't save everyone

As no one is coming to save us, by definition we can't save anyone else from doing this inner work… and why would we? The freedom and confidence we get from this work can be ecstatic and can lead to amazing new vistas and toe-curlingly happy experiences.

What we can do is be kind.

There has been an increased focus on allyship in recent times and I love this. I sometimes marvel that here we are in 2024, and people are still experiencing bias and hate. Whether someone is struggling due to their gender, their sexuality, their race, their disability, their neurodivergence or something else; we can't assume to know how they feel even if we have our own similar experiences.

We can be a nice person though. We can walk alongside them and we can certainly call out other people's unkindness or discrimination. It can feel hard to stand up for someone else but if it is safe to do so, we can speak out, or at least help someone else to get away.

Kindness costs nothing and can be the spark of light in someone's dark day. As Maya Angelou said,

"People will forget what you did and forget what you said, but they

will never forget how you made them feel."

I hope this chapter has given you some work to do, or perhaps you've already done the work and this chapter is a high five moment. Our own energy work is so important. For us to truly feel all that life has to offer, sometimes we have to go through some dark times to fully appreciate the light.

NICKY'S TIPS TO SAVE YOURSELF TIP ELEVEN

Finding love and friendship

If you are feeling lonely, or would like to call in a relationship, start to think about the kind of person you would love to spend time with. If it's a new romantic partner, be sure to include their energy being free for you. Imagine the fun you will have and how this relationship will feel. Then go around your home or office, placing things in twos like ornaments or pictures. Add visual reminders like photos of previous happy times.

(Again thank you Michelle Armitage – you should win a prize for listening!)

CHAPTER TEN
THE BIG VISION

"Our deepest fear is not that we are inadequate.
Our deepest fear is that we are powerful beyond measure.
It is our light, not our darkness, that most frightens us.
We ask ourselves, 'Who am I to be brilliant, gorgeous, talented, fabulous?'
Actually, who are you not to be?
You are a child of God.
Your playing small doesn't serve the world."

A Return To Love, Marianne Williamson

I'm hoping that by now you have realised that I am your biggest cheerleader. I believe in you. I love this Marianne Williamson quote, because sometimes playing small, or playing the role we were told to play, can be the easiest and safest option. When we start to change our outlook and ask for more, we poke the hornets' nest of our own limits and fears but we can also poke the opinions of others, as I mentioned in the last chapter. We can also move into imposter syndrome territory, where we can experience persistent self-doubt and feelings of not being good enough – often in the face of plenty of evidence to the contrary!

In our publishing house, I have lost count of how many authors, when on the threshold of publishing, start to doubt their work. They want to re-write the lot, or worry that what they are saying doesn't make sense, or in my case change the title a week before going to print.

When we choose a different path – in any area of life - it's almost like someone says, "Okay, how badly do you want this?" Our own limiting beliefs can pop up, questions over our body image, whether we're educated of experienced enough, who will be around when we have changed? It can feel daunting.

"Part of being human is being entitled to be happy. We don't need to earn the right, just as we don't need to earn sunlight or oxygen."

I Heart Me, Dr David. R. Hamilton

'Who are you not to be brilliant, gorgeous, talented, fabulous and happy?'

'It is our light, not our darkness that scares us.'

When I was talking to my wonderful friend Kylie Anna, who has a great podcast called Witchy Woo, her spirit team came through to remind me that it's not always our shadow that we are afraid of. Sometimes it can be our light. You see, if you are living in the lightest version of yourself, what then? Does it mean that you always have to be of service to others? Does it mean you can never have a down day? Do you always have to do the right thing and have all of the answers?

The reality is none of these things.

Living in our light means we get to find a balance in life that suits us. We don't magically change everything overnight (I did try to change everything once – it was chaos!). We can, gently and lovingly, make better choices. We can say yes to those things that set our soul on fire, or just give us a nice warm feeling. If something starts to feel yucky, we can change it. If we are doing something we love and then we fall out of love, we can choose again. We do live in a universe of limitless energy and opportunity after all!

We can also accept our humanity. Our ability to get it wrong, to rest when we are tired and to say "That's not for me." We can still have periods where we feel stuck, we can have times that suck...but now we are awake.

We know what is possible for us, and we have a toolkit ready to use.

We have *Bouncebackability*.

Believe me, we may still sulk when something doesn't go our way, or cry when someone hurts us or our loved ones. This planet we reside on is full of harshness, watching the news we can get lost in the suffering and feel powerless. Or we can choose to show up, to do our best to make our own life better and to ripple that energy as far as we are able. Some days we can be brilliant and stun ourselves with our abilities, others we may put the keys in the fridge.

Are you ready to re-visit your vision? This time you can go bigger...

You may have started with a few things you wanted, but what do you *really* want? What is your own vision, uninfluenced by others, unlimited by beliefs? What would make you truly happy?

Maybe it's time to take a notebook to a beautiful place and start to write your new story.

Perhaps you would like to arrange a play day for one and enjoy some you time before settling down to plan your next steps.

Perhaps you need to start with what you no longer want and flip it?

Who are the people that make you smile? Who do you admire? Maybe model some initial ideas on what they do, and then make them your own.

Remember – your vision, your rules.

You could have a spreadsheet filled with experiences and costs. You could have an A1 sheet covered in pictures and words. You may have a simple mind map on an A4 piece of paper - but please, start somewhere.

Also be gentle. In the early days of my personal development, I thought I was attending events with gurus but berated myself for still being stuck in my limited (by me) world. What I didn't realise was, slowly the world was showing me what was possible, by sending me people that had already done the things. I didn't realise that internally I was working through my own beliefs and through holistic therapies and circumstance, I was gradually turning the tables for myself.

As I've stepped into my fifties, I have realised how far I have come, what has become possible and how *unfuckwithable* I actually am. Of course, life still throws curveballs, I miss the obvious, or get so busy that I have to do a massive reset (again). Here are a few hints that may help.

Tweaks not leaps

My friend Kirsty Carr is a woman to be reckoned with, She's an amazing businesswoman and in her own words, hilarious (she really is). She talks about tweaks not leaps, and that's how your vision may play out. Of course, you may find that one day you have done a quantum leap, or your progress may quietly whisper. A teeny step is still forward motion.

Travelling spirals

Sometimes it feels like we are back at square one. Something may occur and you look to the skies and cuss – haven't I dealt with this shit already? Yes, maybe you have. Maybe there's another facet to the energy that was too subtle the first time around. Maybe you needed more energy, or a different attitude to make a new choice. Maybe it just sucks, right? Whatever the circumstance, accept your reality, take a breath and choose to act in a different way this time. Once you step in you may find the path easier and the solution quicker.

Retain your humour

I have learned a lot by being able to laugh at myself. It's a great skill - and I don't mean self-deprecating. Laughing at how life happens sometimes, laughing at my limitations, but in a loving way. Laughter allows us to change the energy around a tough situation, to soften a blow or bring in some light. A really good belly laugh blows away the cobwebs. Recently we were listening to my grandson chuckle and the whole room lit up.

I've added some space here, should you wish to seize the day and write down some thoughts on your vision. I am hoping that you can do the full vision board thing too, but perhaps just start here with a few words or ideas. Remember I am your cheerleader, if you get busy and forget to do this full version for yourself at least you will have a cheat sheet in this book to get you started when you remember!

You could start by using the GROW coaching model

to get a sense of what needs to happen.

GOAL: What are you trying to achieve? Where do you want to be?

REALITY: Without judging yourself or feeling bad, what is your current reality? This will give you an outline of what you want to achieve.

OPTIONS: What could you do to get to your goal? A bit of blue sky thinking to get you into a growth mindset.

WILL: What one thing will you do? Try one thing and see if it works and if not – see your list above.

Here are a few final questions to get you started.

What have I learnt about myself?

……………………………………………………….
……………………………………………………….
……………………………………..……………………
……………………………………………………….
………………………………………………………..
………..……………………………………………………
………………………………………………………..
………………………………………………………..

What will I try first?

……………………………………………………………
……………………………………………………………
……………………………………………………………
……………………………………………………………
……………………………………………………………
……………………………………………………………
……………………………………………………………
……………………………………………………………

As I step into my bright and wonderful future, I would love more…

……………………………………………………………
……………………………………………………………
……………………………………………………………
……………………………………………………………
……………………………………………………………
……………………………………………………………
……………………………………………………………
……………………………………………………………

NICKY'S TIPS TO SAVE YOURSELF
TIP TWELVE

Challenging that negative person in your life

Sometimes our nearest and dearest have negative attitudes which induce the odd eye roll or sigh. If you want to stop the behaviour, take a deep breath and say, "Don't pre-pave my future with your negativity!" Or "Those are your words and you can have them back." It can be very liberating!

CONCLUSION
OUR JOURNEY IS AT AN END

If you have read this far, I am hoping that you are inspired to embark on a plan to become unfuckwithable – or whatever word you would choose! Resilient. Self-reliant. Vivacious. Choose a word that works for you and use it to describe yourself often (even if to start with it's just in your head).

I know the difference that self-care can make, and so armed with your wellbeing plan and your Woo Toolkit I encourage you to create a plan to change your life. I hope that my experiences show that, even when you have had shitty times or circumstances you wouldn't choose, you can bounce back and create a life that is better than you can imagine when you are in the midst of hellish times.

So what are you going to do first? What scares you the most? Perhaps start with a baby step or two, or make one bold move that will make the world sit up and take notice! If you have some tears to shed as you create change, know that it's okay to cry. Tears release the tension we hold in our body and letting that go can only be a good thing.

The thought of saving ourselves can be a daunting one; but lean into that and find the liberation. If you can always save yourself, then the world really is your oyster. It may not always be an easy ride, but the outcome will be worth it. Remember it's okay to get support, but make sure it's in a way that you need rather than a quick fix from someone who doesn't know you well.

And that's it from me; over to you. In the following pages you will find some closing thoughts from Sharon, someone who I love deeply and admire greatly. She has the ability to sum up in a few paragraphs what I've been trying to say in this whole book!

I hope one day I hear from you, to tell me how this book changed your world for the better. And if you're too busy having fun? That will be okay too.

AFTERWORD
BY SHARON CRITCHLOW

Are you ready to do the work? Doing 'the work' is something Nicky and I often talk about, and it is at the heart of saving yourself. In this book you can see how others cannot save you from every feeling and experience you have, as this is what it is to be human. It's no one else's job to mend you and even if they tried to make things right, it is only going to be from their perspective. This book is about living through your trauma, understanding your perspective and making your choices.

Five minutes of listening to yourself is worth more

than five hours of listening to everyone else.

Your perspective is unique to you and the right solution is unique to you, too.

Within these pages you have seen how each trauma or challenge in life is an opportunity to grow and change. This change is the essence of resilience or *BounceBackAbility*. Nicky has shown her own vulnerabilities and how she has grown through those experiences. First from relationship trauma, then physical trauma. If we pay attention to what is happening for us and learn to save ourselves, we are so much better prepared for the next challenge that life presents us with.

This book has come to you for a reason, so embrace it! Try out the Woo Kit ponder on the concepts Nicky explains and make your choices. As Nicky often says – making no decision is a decision in itself. You don't need to commit to doing everything all at once, but do commit to supporting yourself and giving yourself the love, space and understanding you so readily give to others. They say that life is a journey, and so is this book.

ABOUT THE AUTHOR

Nicky is an award winning, international speaker and best-selling author. She's a wife, mum and nanny that lives in Bristol, UK.

At forty years old, Nicky suffered and recovered from a disabling stroke - inspiring a life's mission to make a bigger difference.

Nicky is a mentor, workplace facilitator and keynote speaker, inspiring people to discover their own brand of Bounce. She has helped thousands through her books and keynotes, wellbeing workshops and leadership development in the workplace and her spiritual work and membership under The Witches Brew banner.

Nicky's knowledge, knack for stress-busting and infectious laugh make her an in-demand speaker and she gives the best hugs!

With passion in buckets, Nicky has a unique talent for breaking down the barriers that hold people back from living a bouncy life they absolutely love.

Don't stand too close - her enthusiasm rubs off!

To read about Nicky's keynotes and experience head to: www.nickymarshall.com.

To connect with Nicky on LinkedIn: www.linkedin.com/in/nickymarshall.

ABOUT DISCOVER YOUR BOUNCE

What started as a personal development business in 2013 has grown into a flourishing group of companies! Whether it's publishing your book, working with your team or personal mentoring, we offer frameworks full of practical techniques to provide real support.

Discover Your Bounce Publishing specialises in inspirational stories and business books. We provide writing courses, mentoring for authors and support from inception of your idea through writing, publishing and managing your book launch. If you have an idea for a book, or a part written manuscript that you want to get over the line, contact Nicky or Sharon on the links below.

Discover Your Bounce For Business provides support for employers who want to improve the staff wellbeing, engagement, culture and performance of their business.

We work with CEOs, HR Managers or department heads to deliver workshops with practical, easy to implement techniques that create instant change. As we go to print, we are working with employees across the globe from a variety of industries and have delivered keynotes at some fantastic international conferences and events.

Our Love Your Life programme supports individuals through mentoring and online courses to improve their energy and vision. If your get up and go has got up and gone, get in touch and get bouncing!

Nicky is available to discuss speaking opportunities, wellbeing workshops or private mentoring: www.bit.ly/bookacallwithnicky.

You can also find out more on our website: www.discoveryourbounce.com.

Listen to Nicky and Sharon's podcast: https://linktr.ee/TheMyWellbeingShow.

Join their community: www.facebook.com/groups/discoveryourbouncecommunity

OTHER PERSONAL DEVELOPMENT BOOKS

This little book is the perfect companion for an office desk or a bedside table. It's a perfect, inspiring gift for a friend, or will cheer you up on the gloomiest of days. In this book Nicky and Sharon share short, uplifting tips to help you to live in a more positive way.

Available on Amazon!

Do you love your life? Ever get to the end of the week and realise you haven't done one thing for yourself? Do you have great intentions, but always get side-tracked?
No more!
This gem of a book is your way forward, your way to stick to your plans, to make time for you and to have the energy, wellbeing and amazing life you know you deserve.

With pages to inspire you, places to doodle and monthly inspirations, this is the perfect planner for a bouncy, happy life!

Printed in Great Britain
by Amazon